# Secrets of a Happy Family

# Secrets of a Happy Family

Discover the true meaning of love
through God's plan for the family

by
Deacon Ken & Marie Finn

Copyright © 1996 Deacon Ken and Marie Finn
All rights reserved.

Printed in the United States of America.
Cover Deisgn by Charlotte Johnson
Design and Layout by Jonathon Madrid

Published by St. Dismas Guild
P.O. Box 2129
Escondido CA 92033

Unless otherwise indicated all Scripture citations in this work are taken from the New American Bible. Copyright 1970 by Confraternity of Christian Doctrine.

Second Edition
Second Printing 2001
ISBN 0-9634553-7-0

# CONTENTS

FOREWORD. . . . . . . . . . . . . . . . . . . 11

INTRODUCTION. . . . . . . . . . . . . . . . 17

Chapter 1
GOD'S LOVE. . . . . . . . . . . . . . . . . . . 23

Chapter 2
THE ROLE OF THE MAN. . . . . . . . . . . 49

Chapter 3
THE ROLE OF THE WOMAN. . . . . . . . 75

Chapter 4
THE ROLE OF THE COUPLE. . . . . . . . 99

Chapter 5
THE ROLE OF THE PARENTS. . . . . . . 125

Chapter 6
THE ROLE OF THE CHILDREN. . . . . . 147

Chapter 7
THE ROLE OF THE HOLY SPIRIT. . . . 165

We dedicate this book to
our mother's,
Margaret Rinella & Gertrude Sheehan
who have taught us the value of family and
who were living examples of
looking to others' interests rather than their
own (see Philippians 2:4),
and to our children
Laura, Dan and Gina
whose lives have strongly influenced
our walk with the Lord.

## ACKNOWLEDGEMENTS

Our special thanks to all those who have helped Marie and me in the writing of this book.

To Dick and Ruth Rice and Jean Michaels for their help in editing and arranging of this book, and for their affirmation and support. To Gia Bagaybagayan for all the hours of typing and self-sacrifice. To Paul Blabac and Bob Kloenne for their help on the computer. To our family and friends for their patience, love and support.

We also wish to thank all those persons whose stories we have shared in love and gratitude. Their identities have been changed in the book to protect their privacy.

"There are different gifts but the same Spirit; there are different ministries but the same Lord; there are different works but the same God who accomplishes all of them in everyone" (1 Corinthians 12:4-6).

# Foreword
## Patrick Madrid

In the Gospel of John, we witness an unusual and deeply important conversation between Christ and Simon Peter:

"'Simon, son of John, do you love me more than these?' He said to him, 'Yes, Lord, you know that I love you.' He said to him, 'Feed my lambs.' He then said to him a second time, 'Simon, son of John, do you love me?' He said to him, 'Yes, Lord, you know that I love you.' He said to him, 'Tend my sheep.' He said to him a third time, 'Simon, son of John, do you love me?' Peter was distressed that he had said to him a third time, "Do you love me?' and he said to him, 'Lord, you know everything; you know that I love you.' [Jesus] said to him, 'Feed my sheep'" (John 21:15-17).

You may be wondering why I am introducing a book on the family with this particular Bible passage. The reason is this: In John 21 we see Christ confer upon Simon Peter a special role within his new Family, the Church. He installed Peter in a very important role: to function as the chief shepherd, the one who was specially chosen by the Master to feed, tend, care for, and protect the flock of

*Secrets of a Happy Family*

Christians who would, in each generation, come into the sheepfold of the Church.

In the same way, when a man and a woman unite in the sacrament of holy matrimony, Christ calls to each of them, and in particular to the man, the question: "Do you love me?" Like Simon Peter, their response of "Yes, Lord, you know that we love you," brings about a special new role for them as individuals and as a couple. Out of love for Christ, they are entrusted with a very important mission: to feed, tend, and protect the "lambs" who may be given to them in their children. This little flock, the family, is so precious to God and so worthy of protection and care that he instilled in the sacrament of marriage immense, unfathomable graces that will help the man and woman carry out their new role as husband and wife, father and mother, shepherds to their children.

And just as Christ appointed Peter and the apostles to be shepherds and guardians of the Church family, so too he calls the husband to a unique role of leadership in the family. This leadership, as with Simon Peter, is not one that consists of "lording it over" the wife and children. Nor is it intended to be abused the way a tyrant or a bully might abuse the advantages of his physical size or power. As we see in John 21, Christ intends that the "feeding of his lambs," and the "tending of his sheep," be carried out with love and responsibility, with deep reverence. Why?

Because it is out of love for Christ that husbands are called to love their wives and children. And it's not only because he loves Christ that a man must also love his family. More importantly, I believe, it is precisely because *Christ loves the Church* — each one of us in the flock, singly and as a group — that a husband is called to love and guard his family. In the same way, the wife is also called by Christ to love and care for her husband and children: out of love for Christ, and with Christ's love for the Church as her and her husband's model and pattern.

But how, exactly, should this love of the family be carried out in the day-to-day hurly burly world in which we live? There are so many distractions and worries and challenges that husbands and wives must face each day. There are myriads of parenting theories and fashionable methods for building a marriage and raising children — many of which, sadly, are built on false, selfish premises that lead to false and often supremely unhappy conclusions. The truth about how God wants Christian spouses to build their marriages and, if he should bless them with the gift of children, to feed their lambs, is often drowned out by the cacophony of competing voices in our world today that cry out for our attention, clamoring for you to follow after this or that theory that happens to be in vogue today.

Turn away from the din. Quiet your heart and explore in the pages of this wonderful book, the wisdom of God

*Secrets of a Happy Family*

for the family. In these pages, Deacon Ken Finn and his wife Marie — parents of a large and happy family — unfold for you the singular blueprint for God has laid out for successful marriages in His written Word and in the two-thousand year wisdom of the ancient Church. They unlock for you the secrets of a happy family. Their years of wise and loving obedience to God's plan for the family is reflected in this book. Their advice will not tantalize you with unattainable "perfectionism" or unrealistic ideals too hard to follow in "real life." No. They show you here, simply and without pretense, how following God's plan for marriage will liberate you and your spouse from confusion and uncertainty about how you should best love one another and raise your children.

Following God's plan and seeking his will is *the* secret to any truly happy marriage and family. In this book, Deacon Ken and Marie will reveal that secret to you and show you, step by step, how to make it come alive in your own marriage and family.

Patrick Madrid, author of *Surprised by Truth* and *Search and Rescue*. Spring, 2001

# St. Dismas Guild

This book was written under the auspices of St. Dismas Guild. St. Dismas Guild is a non-profit organization supported by donations only. The guild distributes the *Bread of Life Catholic Bible Study,* Bibles, catechisms, religious pamphlets, rosaries and other religious items to individuals, parishes, prisons, missions, and the poor all over the world. A major part of the work of St. Dismas Guild is in prison ministry. For all our materials there is no charge.

The Guild's goal is to influence people to seek and know God our Father through His Son Jesus Christ, by reading the Word of God with the understanding that the Holy Spirit resides in them, teaching and reminding them of all that Jesus says and does. "The Advocate, the Holy Spirit that the Father will send in my name, He will teach you everything and remind you of all that I told you" (John 14:26).

The Scripture text that sums up the ministry of St. Dismas Guild is this: "Go rather to the lost sheep of the house of Israel. As you go, make this proclamation: The kingdom of heaven is at hand. Cure the sick, raise the dead, cleanse lepers, drive out demons. Without cost you have received; without cost you are to give" (Matthew 10:6-8).

*Secrets of a Happy Family*

For further information please contact: St. Dismas Guild, P.O. Box 2129, Escondido, CA 92033; phone: 760/751-8541; fax. 760/751 8505; e-mail: benedictus1@aol.com; www.stdismas.org.

# Introduction

> "I want you to know that
> the head of every man is Christ;
> the head of a woman is her husband;
> and the head of Chrst is the Father."
>
> 1 Corinthians 11:3

The theme for this book, God's plan for the family, came to us as a fruit of prayer, the best place for such a book to find its beginning. The work has also been the fruit of considerable experience: We've been married forty years and have three children and eight grandchildren. Meanwhile, we've both been in family ministry for more than twenty years. Ken was also a full-time prison chaplain for twelve years, while Marie has been a Scripture study teacher for many years.

*The Bread of Life Catholic Bible Study*, which we co-authored, is now being used in many countries around the world. We've also conducted seminars on the family in Colorado, Texas and other areas in the southwestern U.S. This volume is a development of selected material originally presented in these and related seminars.

Over the years our personal relationship with God and with each other has grown deeper as a result of being committed to the Word of God and obedient to the Church's teaching. This has come about through our daily prayer, reading the Word of God, reflecting, listening and being obedient to His Word under the guidance of the Holy Spirit and the Church.

Throughout this book we've attempted to provide a solid biblical background for understanding God's plan for the functions, roles and relationships of those who make up the family. We discuss how God has loved us and how we must love one another; how men are called to be the spiritual leaders in the family, while women are called to be the affirmers and comforters of others; how couples are to be united as one in Christ and, as co-creators, how they should view their parental responsibilities; how children are to be obedient to parents, and parents, as children of God, are to be obedient to their Heavenly Father. The last chapter deals with how the Holy Spirit sanctifies, teaches, comforts and empowers us.

Of greatest importance is the personal relationship between *you* and *God*. This personal relationship with God is essential before you can experience a true, personal, intimate relationship with others. Ephesians 5:21 says, "Be subordinate to one another out of reverence for Christ."

Why are so many families not living according to God's standard of moral and marital laws? Because they're not following the lead of the Holy Spirit. It's one thing to re-

*Introduction*

ceive the Holy Spirit at baptism, yet another to be following the lead of the Holy Spirit. Ephesians 5:18 says, "Be filled with the Spirit," and John 1:39 says, "Come and see."

The Christian family is many times referred to as the domestic Church. In its original form it's made up of a husband and wife who are called to give themselves in love and in the gift of life. From this small community the individual can learn moral values and begin to honor God, family and country. The family is called to be responsible for all its members—young, old, sick, handicapped, and poor. Families are thus the lifeblood of all societies.

The core of the Christian family is the father and mother, who are called to a covenant relationship of marriage. The matrimonial covenant is about a man and a woman establishing between themselves a partnership. This marriage covenant is based on their giving of themselves to each other and on the procreation of offspring. Christ has raised the marriage covenant to the dignity of a sacrament, and that's what this book is all about.

In the process of writing we've grown spiritually and received many healings from the Lord. The Holy Spirit is our Teacher, and we've learned most of all to lean on Him, to listen to Him, and to follow His advice.

At times, it hasn't been easy deferring to one another, but the rewards have been great. As we are told in Scripture (see James 5:16), we're called to confess our sins to

*Secrets of a Happy Family*

one another so that we may be healed. We've learned not to rely on our own understanding, but to rely on God.

First thing every morning we spend quiet time with the Lord individually, praying, listening and trying to obey His lead. As we follow His lead we've become one in mind and heart.

As you read this book, our prayer for you is that you come to know the deep love of God for you personally and that you come to know and recognize the Holy Spirit in the midst of your everyday life. We also pray that you may be healed in body, mind and spirit. We humbly offer this book as a guide to help you respond to the invitation of the Holy Spirit to become a Spirit-filled family following Christ in our time.

# Secrets of a Happy Family

# CHAPTER ONE
# GOD'S LOVE

"Yes, God so loved the world that He gave His only Son, that whoever believes in Him may not die but may have eternal life" (John 3:16). God loved us so much that He sent His Son to die for us—to free us from Satan's hold on us, which includes sin, sickness and death (see Isaiah 53). Our response to this sacrifice shows in our relationships with one another. We hope it will become clear as you read this book that we cannot have the same love relationship with others that God has with us unless we accept His love, experience His love and abide in Him.

Pope John Paul II states: "Without love the family is not a community of persons and, in the same way, without love the family cannot live, grow and perfect itself as a community of persons."[1] "Man cannot live without love. He remains a being that is incomprehensible for himself, his life is senseless, if love is not revealed to him, if he does not encounter love, if he does not experience it and make it his own, if he does not participate intimately in it."[2]

## Proof of God's Love (the Son)

How did God prove His love for us? "It is precisely in

*Secrets of a Happy Family*

this that God proves his love for us: that while we were still sinners, Christ died for us" (Romans 5:8). We're separated from the Father when we live the way we think is best for us without first submitting to Him. Jesus shows us over and over how to love by His example of submitting Himself completely to His Father's will. He did everything in obedience to His Father. Ultimately He submitted to His Father's will and died on the cross (see Luke 22:42).

The Lord tells us over and over how much He loves us. For example, 1 John 4:8 tells us that "God is love," then verses 9 and 10 go on to say, "God's love was revealed in our midst in this way: He sent His only Son to the world that we might have life through Him. Love, then, consist in this: not that we have loved God, but that He has loved us and has sent His Son as an offering for our sins."

Bill was a man who had not experienced the love of God for him personally until he had been in prison. He felt there must be something more than what he was experiencing in life. Bill's whole life had been one of searching for acceptance and love and purpose. He got involved in using and selling drugs and consequently was in and out of prison.

Bill went to a Christian rehab program for alcoholics and drug addicts, based on freedom from substance abuse through Scripture. There he learned that Jesus Christ was

*God's Love*

the "Higher Power" often spoken of by rehab programs, and that healing could only come through Him. The program was successful. He came to know the love of God personally for him and repented of all his wrongdoing.

Bill moved away to another state, but unfortunately fell back into his old lifestyle and eventually ended up back in prison. Today, in a federal prison, Bill has returned to the Lord once more, and the Lord is working powerfully through him as he shares how God has saved him from his old way of life and as he leads the *Bread of Life Catholic Bible Study*. He knows God loves him, not for anything he did or didn' t do, but because Jesus died on the cross for him.

We find in God's Word how much He loves us and how much He has sacrificed Himself for us. To understand better that kind of selfless sacrifice, we can look at a certain mother who sacrificed herself so her son could live.

Peg's son was born crippled at birth. He couldn't sit up or even crawl. Although Peg was told that her son would never walk, she had faith in God and gave of herself to her son. She spent years in training him to move into different positions and paid for countless surgeries to be performed on the boy. Spending much of his life in a body cast, her son has been totally dependent on his mother. Peg's faith has been not only her strength, but her son's strength, too.

Peg shows us the difference between an adult and a child. An adult gives and a child takes. Jesus tells us to

*Secrets of a Happy Family*

love one another as He has loved us (see John 13:34). He reveals to us how we're capable of loving others because He has loved us first (see 1 John 4:19).

We show love to others in the same way Christ did for us. He loved us first not only to save us, but to show us how to love others. He tells us in John 15:12, "Love one another as I have loved you."

In obeying this commandment, we're proving how much we love God. As we die to our own personal need for love, and draw that love from God to fill others' need for love, we're not only in obedience to God's commandments; we also become recipients of the fullness and completeness of God's unlimited love. Jesus said, "Anyone who loves me will be true to my word, and my Father will love him; we will come to him and make our dwelling place with him." (see John 14:23).

We cannot truly love one another until we *first experience God's love* for us. Scripture tells us: "Yes, God so loved the world that He gave His only begotten Son that whoever believes in Him may not die but may have eternal life" (John 3:16). God is offering to each one of us a full share in His family. He's allowing us to become heirs of His kingdom by believing and accepting His Son, Jesus.

God's love and generosity are so incredible that he allowed His Son, Jesus, who had committed no sin Him-

*God's Love*

self, to be tortured and slaughtered for the sins of all the people in the world. His blood washed us clean, and because of what *He* did, we became eligible to live with Him in eternity. In fact, if there were no one else but you, He still would have gone on that cross to free you because He loves you.

Jesus died for each one of us because He loves each one of us so much. We can only truly love others when we realize how much we're loved by Him and *accept* that love. "God proves His love for us in that while we were still sinners Christ died for us" (Romans 5:8). As Pope John Paul II has noted: "The Spirit which the Lord pours forth gives a new heart, and renders man and woman capable of loving one another as Christ has loved us."[3]

Ken was born with a serious lung disease. He spent much of his childhood in and out of hospitals. He was deeply afraid of pain and death. He thought God was a stern Judge who punished you if you were bad.

Ken attended church many times with his mother, praying for a healing. He's grateful to his parents for handing down to him their faith and sending him to a Catholic grade school where he was taught about God's love for him. But it took years before he truly felt that love.

In his late twenties, Ken had a lung operation that developed serious complications. During one particularly bad episode it was feared he might not survive the night.

At that time he and Marie had a ten-month-old baby, and he didn't want to die.

Panic-stricken and not knowing what to do, Ken prayed to God and promised that if God would let him live, he would dedicate his life to Him. Once he survived, Ken spent many years trying to live up to that bargain, although he still feared that if he wasn't pleasing God, he would be punished. He was actually trying to work his way to heaven through good deeds.

Ken would watch Marie get up early each morning to pray and read Scripture. He was jealous of the attention that God was receiving from her and envious that she was getting stronger in her faith day by day. She seemed radiant when she came out of her room after prayer or Bible study. Ken was curious about a God who could bring about such a change in a person.

His marriage looked good on the surface, but it was in reality a contract of legalism: Most all his actions were not done from the heart, but merely to conform to the law of the Church. Ken set the highest expectations for himself and held the same expectations for his wife and children.

After Marie introduced him to a Bible study, and as he became steeped in the Word of God, Ken's life began to change dramatically. He learned that God loved him with no strings attached, no laws, no rules. God loved him just as he was, not for what he did, but for what Jesus did, who died for us because He loved everyone in the whole world. The more he learned about Jesus, the more he changed.

The Scripture revealed to Ken that much of his concept of God was totally distorted. He had believed in a God only to be feared and yet found a God of love and mercy. As Ken realized how much God loved him, he began to love others more freely and his level of trust rose dramatically.

Ken's love for God has affected his marriage deeply. God's Word revealed to him that he didn't know how to love a woman, and then Jesus showed him how to love through God's Word. Ken still has a lung disease, but he is in the process of being healed physically, emotionally and spiritually. When he realized that God died to save him, not to kill him, then he knew that one day he would be healed forever.

Christ tells us in Scripture He has a plan for our life: "I came that they might have life and have it abundantly" (John 10:10). In order to have this abundant life we must become *holy*—but we first have to become *whole*. We must physically, emotionally and spiritually experience the reality of Jesus and the power of the Holy Spirit transforming and changing our whole lives.

How does this happen? By our submitting to what God is saying, and then living our lives according to His Word. When we submit and listen to the Holy Spirit, He teaches us and reminds us of all Jesus said and did.

When we don't submit to God, we rebel. Rebellion is doing things our way instead of listening and acting on what God is saying. You can spot rebellion in a person by a simple test. A rebellious person will not take responsibility for his or her actions and, instead of being accountable, will invariably blame others.

Marie was once a shy, reserved girl looking to her parents for guidance and direction for her life. They gave her the guidance she desired, along with stability and security. She learned from her training at church of a God who loved her if she did all the right things.

But Marie also believed that if she did something wrong, God would punish her, and if she was really bad, He would send her to hell to burn forever. So she grew up trying to please Him and everyone else out of fear. She was always looking to others to fill her need for love as well.

When Marie married Ken she brought this same attitude into her marriage and passed it on to her children. She would try so hard to be good and please her husband and children that she became a perfectionist. Because she thought no one could do things as well as she could, she did all the work, while searching to have someone meet her need to be loved.

Even at church gatherings, it always seemed to Marie that others were getting all the attention and she was on

*God's Love*

the outside looking in. Over the years she grew depressed, full of bitterness, anger, and rage toward herself and others. She grew critical of others because she thought they couldn't do anything right. She hated herself and didn't want to go on feeling this way.

One day, depressed and crying, she read in the Bible that love was patient and kind, it wasn't self-seeking or prone to anger, and it did not brood over injuries (see 1 Corinthians 13). Miraculously, Marie saw herself for who she was. She wasn't patient and kind; she didn't know how to love; and she couldn't stop doing what she was doing.

She confessed to God that she didn't know how to love, and it made her miserable. Only when she acknowledged her sinfulness was she able to yield herself to God to experience the power of His love and forgiveness. Until then, she didn't realize that *she herself* was responsible for her impatience, brooding, and critical spirit.

That day, God took all Marie's emptiness and depression and filled her with His love and forgiveness. It was nothing she could have done for herself; it was what He did for her. She did not choose Him; He chose her (see John 15:16).

Marie learned what the psalmist meant when he wrote: "As long as I would not speak, my bones wasted away with my groaning all the day. For day and night your hand was heavy upon me; my strength was dried up as by the heat of

*Secrets of a Happy Family*

summer. Then I acknowledged my sin to you, my guilt I covered not. I said, 'I confess my faults to the Lord,' and you took away the guilt of my sin" (Psalm 32:3-5). When Marie looks back now, she can see how long it took to realize fully that even while she was still sinning, the Lord died for her (see Romans 5:8).

God told Marie that He loved her and He would teach her how to love. "I will instruct you and show you the way you should walk; I will counsel you, keeping my eye on you" (Psalm 32:8). She then realized what it meant that God loved her by sending His Son, Jesus, to die on a cross for her. He took her sin from her on the cross.

Jesus made her feel so good. She felt special to Him and no longer afraid of Him. From that day on, she has wanted to learn everything about Him that she can. She spends time every day in prayer with Him and reading His Word.

John 14:26 has become Marie's prayer every time she reads His Word: "But the Counselor, the Holy Spirit, whom the Father will send in my name, He will teach you all things, and bring to your remembrance all that I have said to you." Jesus is her Teacher; His Spirit resides in her and will lead her to all truth. The more His Spirit leads her to the truth of her Father, the more she feels loved by Him and feels special.

Once Marie became convinced of God's love, she

*God's Love*

stopped demanding that others love her, because she felt loved by Him. She stopped looking to be loved and started loving with the love He gave her. Marie's fear of doing wrong and getting punished left her. God tells her when she is wrong; she then confesses and feels tremendously loved by Him. He will always forgive her and welcome her back into His loving arms.

Sin is a rupture in the relationship between God and man. Romans 1:28-29 says, "They did not see fit to acknowledge God, so God delivered them up to their own depraved sense to do what is unseemly. They are filled with every kind of wickedness; maliciousness, greed, ill will, envy, murder, bickering, deceit, craftiness. They are gossips. . . ." All these things separate us from God.

St. Maximillian Kolbe was a Polish prisoner in the German concentration camp at Auschwitz, Poland, during World War II. He served as a Catholic priest of the Franciscan order. One day a prison break was attempted, and the guards imposed the penalty that ten prisoners would be selected at random and killed.

The men were standing in order as each one's name was called. The prisoner in front of Fr. Kolbe was a young man with several children. Fr. Kolbe stepped forward and stated that he was single and had no children, so he was requesting that he be taken instead of the young married man.

The commander shrugged as if to scoff, but he accepted the offer. The ten victims, including Fr. Kolbe, were confined to a dismal cell; eventually all of them either died from starvation or were executed by injection. In this way, St. Maximillian showed us that loving one another as Jesus loved us can mean laying down our lives for one another.

Jesus Christ is the only way that man can live the abundant life and know and experience God's love and plan for his life. We look to Scripture to see how and why He died in our place. He demonstrated how much He loved us by dying for us while we were still rejecting Him.

Sadly, today there are still people who could care less that God demonstrated His love for them in that, while they were still sinners, Christ died for them (see Romans 5:8). He paid the ransom for our sins with His death on the cross. His death was a pardon for all our crimes. Because of what He did, you and I became not ex-convicts, but forgiven free men and women.

## The Activity of God's Love (the Holy Spirit)

God is offering us a personal relationship with His Son, Jesus. He loves us, He wants to be with us, and He has given His Spirit to those who accept His invitation. Once we have accepted His invitation, His Spirit dwells within us so that we might be more closely united to Him than we are to anyone or anything else. *Our love for each other is a direct*

*God's Love*

*reflection of our awareness of how much God loves us.* Until we have that awareness, we are not capable of truly loving another person. We cannot love God and hate our brother (see 1 John 4:20-21).

The Holy Spirit teaches us every day by the words and example of Jesus Christ how to love: through reading God's Word, through caring for the poor, through dying to self, and through following the teachings of the Church. As we're stripped of self, and we put on Christ, we come to understand the *true* meaning of love. For God so loved the world He gave His only Son, to teach us by His life here on earth how to love.

He gave His beloved only Son to be tortured and crucified on our behalf because He loves us so much. His beloved Son gave up His life in obedience to His Father because He loves us so much. The Holy Spirit loves us so much that He teaches all truth and reminds us of all Jesus said and did.

Scripture tells us that Jesus thirsts for us (see John 19:28, Psalm 143:6), and He wants to have a personal relationship with us, far more than we ourselves want such a relationship with Him. Our Lord thirsts not for water, but for something much greater; that is, to love us and to be loved by us. This is what the Good News is all about.

God not only loves us; He also forgives us all our sins. We too thirst to be loved and to love others. Jesus has

## Secrets of a Happy Family

filled us with life-giving water to satisfy that thirst. We fill His thirst by abiding in Him. With the overflow of love He pours into our hearts, we're then capable of loving others. The Holy Spirit will help us grow into a mature relationship with Jesus, simply because He thirsts for us.

In the *Bread of Life Catholic Bible Study,* we ask an important question: "What two things must we do in order to receive the Holy Spirit?" Jesus says, "You may *ask* me anything in my name and I will do it. If you love me, you will *obey* my command" (see John 14:14-15). You must ask, but you must also *listen* to what he says, and obey.

How do we know whether we're listening to Him, or to ourselves, or to others, or to Satan? If what we hear is in conformity to Scripture, we know we're listening to Him. That's why it's so important to come to know Him personally through His Spirit and through His Word. The Bible teaches us what Jesus said when He walked the earth.

Ann is a small, attractive woman who will be spending the rest of her life in prison. She tells how she was once such a bad mother that if she were one of her kids, she would hate her mother as much as they do. Her life was filled with drugs, violence, and continued self-humiliation. Tossed around from one gang member to another, she finally landed in prison.

But there Ann found Christ. Now she's open, gentle, and at peace with herself. Christ loves her without any angles or conditions. He comforts her in times of loneliness and affirms her when she does good. As she herself will tell you, the old Ann is dead, and the new Ann has a new life in Jesus Christ, even in prison.

We can enter into a relationship with God through our baptism. In baptism we receive the Father, the Son and the Holy Spirit, and Scripture tells us that when we receive the Spirit, we also receive power (see Acts 1:8). It's the power of the Holy Spirit working through our acceptance of Him that frees us to experience personally the life-giving love of Jesus Christ.

# The Application of God's Love

## Our need for God

You might ask, "Why do I need God to know how to love?" We need God because most of us look to other human beings to fill our need for love. Yet no matter how hard they try, they can never completely fill that need for love. The only way a person can truly love is by accepting the love that God has poured out upon us through His beloved Son on the cross.

We become more and more angry and resentful toward others when we expect them to love us the way Christ loves us, which is impossible because of their fallen human nature. Depression is one of the clearest signs of this

*Secrets of a Happy Family*

anger turned inward. We sometimes brood for days over the smallest things, such as a spouse's forgetting to call or do something that we requested. We don't say we're sorry for being angry because we think they're wrong, while anger, bitterness and depression may still consume us.

If we find ourselves with such problems, we should be glad to know that lives have been changed tremendously through the power of God's Word convicting, teaching and training us in right living. The Word of God is like a mirror. Our lives can really change if we look into it, repent and submit totally to living God's way rather than the world's way.

The well-known "love chapter" of the Bible, 1 Corinthians 13, is a good scriptural text to help us discern whether we've accepted and received God's love for us. Through this passage, our whole understanding of what it means to love can be changed. God's Word makes us look at ourselves as we really are.

Are we patient, or are we impatient? Are we kind, or are we mean and say unkind things to one another? Do we see only faults, remaining blind to all the good others do to show their love? Are we constantly brooding over injuries? Are we self-seeking, adding up all we do for others to compare it to what they do for us?

Take Al as an example of what we're talking about. Al used to complain frequently that his wife wasn't filling his need for love sexually. He insisted that she was cold and unresponsive to him. When he shared this problem with another woman, she responded to him and began filling that need in him. He eventually divorced his wife and married the other woman.

Al may have a new partner, yet today his problem remains the same: He's still trying to have his needs met by another human being. He's refusing to repent. He doesn't see how he's refusing to love as Jesus loved, which means dying to himself and looking to the needs of others. He doesn't yet understand that love is not taking; love is giving.

When Al sees and repents of the harm he did to his ex-wife, he'll then be opening the door to allow God's love to come in. But in the meantime he's still refusing God's invitation by not repenting.

Jesus is knocking at the door of your heart as well. Are you listening?

## Separation from God

We separate ourselves from God's presence through sin in our lives. Romans 3:23 says, "All men have sinned and are deprived of the glory of God." If our relationship with God is strained or filled with tension, our relationship with others will also be strained and filled with tension.

Scripture tells us as well that the wages of sin is death

*Secrets of a Happy Family*

(see Romans 6:23). Sin always causes spiritual separation from God. We need only look again at Scripture to see that because of Adam and Eve's sin, they were removed from the garden of Eden and eventually died (see Genesis chapter 3). Satan led them into sin; because of him sin, sickness and death became the order of the day.

As we've already noted, some of us have been raised to see God merely as a keeper of rules. We think that if we break those rules, God won't love us and we may not get to heaven. So we go through life being and doing good for the wrong reasons.

Many times the primary reason for our obedience is *fear*. But when we accept and receive the love God has for us and recognize His presence in us, the fear leaves. Perfect love casts out fear because fear has to do with punishment (see 1 John 4:18). We're no longer afraid of punishment, which is a fear of death, because we believe that Jesus' death on the cross saved us from that fear and offers us eternal life.

Think of St. Ignatius of Antioch, a second-century bishop and martyr. He faced being thrown to ravenous wild beasts in the arena because he refused to give homage to the emperor as a god. His friend pleaded with him to agree with the emperor that he was in error. But Ignatius stated that torture and death held no fear for him, because he knew he wasn't being punished by God. He knew the love

*God's Love*

God had for him made him stronger in facing the punishment of man. St. Ignatius had love, not fear, even in death.

## Repentance

The Word of God is sharper than any two-edged sword; it truly divides and cuts between bone and marrow (see Hebrews 4:12). It's like a hammer that crushes rock (see Jeremiah 23:29). It opens our eyes to see the truth, and the truth sets us free (see John 8:32). Before you can be born anew, or born of the Holy Spirit, you must be convicted, confess, and then come into repentance, which means change.

St. John the Baptist preached, "Repent," and in that way he made ready the way of the Lord. When Jesus came, He preached the same thing: "Repent and believe" (see Mark 1:1-14).

As a wealthy young man, St. Francis of Assisi encountered a horribly disfigured leper. He was repulsed and anxious to get away from the pathetic figure. Francis thanked God that he himself was not poor, disfigured, and a total nobody. This young man was in rebellion; his high-spirited, self-gratifying lifestyle revealed that he was primarily concerned with himself and his friends.

Then in a moment of reflection, Francis saw himself as he really was. He thought about that horrible-looking leper, and repentance came into his heart—that is, he had

*Secrets of a Happy Family*

a change of heart. He knew God wanted him to change his attitude and lifestyle. So he raced back to the disfigured leper and not only embraced him but also kissed him. He saw Jesus behind the disguise of scars and filth. We too are to see Jesus in the disguise of others.

God's Word opens our eyes to the truth about ourselves and brings us to confess our sin. Faith follows and continues to grow through the abiding Word of God. Our life's journey then begins in submission and fellowship with the Holy Spirit, and the excitement of this new life continues.

Jesus showed us how to die to ourselves—that is, how to empty ourselves of ego—for a greater gain, primarily everlasting life with Him, as well as peace of heart and mind on this earth. He thirsts for us to love Him forever (see John 19:28). He's waiting for the day we'll come to Him and say, "I want to be with you."

St. Dismas, the thief who hung on the cross that was next to Jesus' cross, recognized his own guilt and sinfulness. He saw that Jesus was undeserving of what was happening to Him. The thief on the other side of Jesus, however, refused to see himself for who he was and really didn't care what was happening to Jesus. The other thief wanted to be free to continue living as he always had.

Dismas asked Jesus to remember him when He came into His kingdom. Jesus told him He would be with him

*God's Love*

that day in paradise. He set Dismas free. We too can be free by acknowledging our guilt and accepting God's invitation to be with Him.

Scripture tells us that when we call out to God, He not only listens, but also comes to us if we seek Him with all our hearts (see Jeremiah 29:12-13). He promises us a life-changing experience when we allow Him to become the Lord of our lives. When that happens, we become capable of loving others as a result of the experience of being loved by Him. We can expect great things when we open ourselves to God's love.

## Hope

Christ died for us, even while we were sinning (see Romans 5:8). He openly, unhesitatingly and unconditionally gave up His life for us, so we would be free to choose life or death. Because of His love, we can have hope.

Joan is a woman who knows about hope. She's married and prays constantly for her husband and three adult children. Her husband frequently travels to another country to be with another woman. Both her husband and her children abuse her verbally.

Nevertheless, Joan knows beyond a doubt that she is loved by God, and that knowledge allows her to bear up under these circumstances, totally relying on the Lord. When she's alone with the Lord, crying out in her pain, He com-

*Secrets of a Happy Family*

forts her and tells her not to condemn her husband. She constantly asks the Lord for help to live under these conditions while she chooses a life with God.

Joan is hoping firmly that her family will turn to the Lord. She sincerely believes that without her obedience to what God tells her in prayer, she could not love in this manner and would be without the overflow of His healing love for her. Without the Lord, she would have no hope.

Jesus let His blood be shed in order to wash us free of sin. Is there a limit to His love for us? The answer is *no*. When we realize how much He has done for us, we have just a glimpse of how much He loves us. We are then ready to enter into a deeper personal relationship with Him. We become capable of loving others simply because we know, that we know, that we know, that we are loved by Him first (see 1 John 4:19), just as Joan knows.

Love is not a warm, fuzzy feeling. Love is a decision that many times causes great discomfort. It's a decision that always includes a sacrifice. It's a decision to die to self in order to fill another's need for love. Love isn't easy.

Read the account of Jesus' agony in the Garden of Gethsemane, which ended with His prayer that not His will, but his Father's will, would be done (see Matthew 26:36-39). We receive our love from Him in the time we

*God's Love*

spend alone with Him. This is time communicating with Him, both speaking and listening to Him. This time makes us capable of loving others even when they are not loving us, just as Jesus did on the cross.

To love others is to let them experience our mercy and kindness. *We must always remember that mercy is for those who don't deserve it.* Love is a realistic appraisal of the situation followed by a sacrificial choice that affects other people. Joan, for example, is merciful to her cheating husband, even though he doesn't deserve it.

God's love is always available to us, and God is always waiting to forgive us. Just as we must always remember that love is not an emotion but a decision, we must also keep in mind that forgiveness, too, is not an emotion, but a decision.

God loves us so much that when He created us, He gave us the greatest gift of all—free will. This gift is the ultimate sign of how much God loves us. He loves each one of us enough to let us determine our own course of action. We make our own choices, good or bad.

God constantly forgives us when we repent of making the wrong choice. He gives us the chance to say, "I'm sorry for making such a bad choice; I'm sorry for hurting my fellow man, myself, and you, Lord." He's a God who loves us so much that He chose His only-begotten Son to pay the price for all the bad choices made by everyone who

*Secrets of a Happy Family*

ever lived.

We're able to choose our own path, whether it's good or evil. As an example of what we're talking about, consider Paul, a young man from a good, solid family, who chose to dabble in drugs. Soon the drugs were in control of Paul. One bad decision followed another, and he was headed for state prison.

Paul was given a chance to go to a rehab center as an alternative sentence. He chose to be open to the prayer and Bible study at the center. He also chose to open the door of his heart and let Christ come in (see Revelation 3:20). Today, Paul is reunited with his family and has a fine job, simply because of his choice to let Christ be in charge of his life.

God continues giving us His love by leaving us His Holy Spirit, who makes us holy and empowers us in our journey through His kingdom back to our home in heaven with Him.

*God's Love*

## Questions for Reflection

- How am I experiencing God's love in my life?
- How are my relationships with those close to me separating me from God?
- How do I need to repent in order to experience in a deep personal way God's love for me?

## Application of the Lesson

*Romans 5:8:* "…God proves His love for us; that while we were still sinners, Christ died for us."

Watch for areas where you can die to yourself by not doing what you want and meeting your own needs, but instead meeting the needs of another person, such as your spouse or the person closest to you.

Give your spouse a specific proof of your love. Let us pray:

Father, I'm a sinner. I'm sorry for all those I've hurt. Jesus, thank You for dying on the cross and forgiving me. I commit my life to You. I desire from this day forth to do Your will. Amen.

Now that we've talked about what God's love is, we'll go on to describe the role of the man, woman, couple and children in God's divine order.

## CHAPTER TWO
# THE ROLE OF THE MAN
## *Insights From Ken*

We've been taught that the foundation of the whole human race is the family. Traditionally, we've also been taught that the foundation of the family is the father, who has the place of honor. The father has the right to expect respect and obedience from his family.

Our Holy Father Pope John Paul II speaks of the father's role this way: "In revealing and in reliving on earth the very fatherhood of God,[4] a man is called upon to ensure the harmonious and united development of all the members of the family: He will perform this task by exercising generous responsibility for the life conceived under the heart of the mother, by a more solicitous commitment to education, a task he shares with his wife,[5] by work which is never a cause of division in the family but promotes its unity and stability, and by means of the witness he gives of an adult Christian life which effectively introduces the children into the living experience of Christ and the church."[6]

## Scriptural Authority for Leadership

The *scriptural* description of the man's role begins with God's telling Adam that he's to have dominion over all things and creatures in the garden. Scripture tells us that God took the man and settled him in the Garden of Eden to cultivate and care for it (see Genesis 2:15). From this verse we're able to see that God created man first and established him as a leader over all creation.

God then gave the man headship over the garden and eventually over the woman, whom he had not yet created. Adam was made the chief steward of all God's creation. He also was given the responsibility of being accountable for all that took place in the garden. This concept must be grasped if we're to accept the scriptural basis for the headship role of the male.

God gave man this order: "You are free to eat from any of the trees in the garden except the tree of knowledge of good and bad. From that tree you shall not eat; the moment you eat from it you are surely doomed to die" (Genesis 2:16-17).

God spoke directly to Adam and gave him the terms of His command. He told Adam what was expected of him; the limits of his authority and areas of his responsibility were clearly defined. And He gave Adam a *free will* so that he might have the freedom to *choose obedience* and *live* forever, or to *choose_disobedience* and *die* (see Deuteronomy 30:19).

*The Role of the Man*

Adam was told by God what the plan was before Eve was created. This role of headship came natural for the man. It was part of his nature to cultivate and care for all that God had given him. That's why the man who's obedient to God's commands is a true leader.

## Traditional Functions

The *traditional* role of the man was as main provider and protector of the family. This role goes back to Adam. Men were called to work outside of the home as hunters, fishermen, farmers, and other occupations.

A man has always been associated with what he does. When a man has no job, he loses a part of his inner being. He needs to be the caretaker, protector and provider of his family. This is part of his nature as originally given by God to Adam. Man has always been called to be a worker and a leader.

In the Apostolic Exhortation *On the Family,* Pope John Paul II says: "Love for his wife as mother of their children and love for the children themselves are for the man the natural way of understanding and fulfilling his own fatherhood. Above all where social and cultural conditions so easily encourage a father to be less concerned with his family or at any rate less involved in the work of education, efforts must be made to restore socially the conviction that the place and task of the father in and for the family is of unique and irreplaceable importance" (n. 25).

## Provider

In the past, the man was responsible for providing shelter against adverse weather conditions, wild animals, and other threats to his family's health and safety. The husband delegated his authority to his wife or an older son when he had to be away from the home for a lengthy time. That authority was to be respected as if the husband himself were present. The role of the male in leadership was also to provide education for his children, and he many times delegated this authority to his wife.

Marie's father, for example, took care of his five children in the same way his father before him had cared for his family. He owned a grocery store and worked seven days a week to put shoes on the children's feet and give them whatever else they needed. He was a hard worker, and while Marie's mother never worked outside the home, the household responsibilities fell to her. Her father never used credit cards and only allowed himself to purchase what he could pay for immediately.

When Marie married me, I provided for her in much the same way her father had. I had a secure job while she stayed home and took care of the children and household.

*The Role of the Man*

## Protector

In the past, the man was also responsible for those who were under his protection when they were led into sins such as envy, greed, and keeping up with the Joneses. We see this clearly in Adam's situation. He could have stopped the ongoing debate between the serpent and Eve (see Genesis 3:1-6) immediately if he had obeyed God's command to him, which was not to eat from the tree of the knowledge of good and bad (see Genesis 2:16-17).

Keep in mind that God had given the command to Adam *directly* and not to Eve. Adam probably had told Eve not to eat from the tree, because she knew about the command. Yet he was the one made to accept full responsibility for the disobedience of them both, and that's the price of *headship*.

## Suitability of Partner

God saw that after the man named all the different birds and animals, he still was lonely and incomplete. Adam needed a helpmate to make him complete. The Lord God then built up into a woman the rib he had taken from the man (see Genesis 2:22).

The man said: "This one, at last, is bone of my bones and flesh of my flesh; this one shall be called 'woman,' for out of 'her man' this one has been taken" (Genesis 2:23).

*Secrets of a Happy Family*

Adam called her "woman," which means "from man," and was able truly to declare that she came not just from his rib, but also from his bones and his flesh. He was made out of the clay, she was made out of him. He was to be her leader, she his helpmate.

A man needs a woman's companionship, and he needs her as a partner in creation. A man's suitable partner is one with him in harmony with his Creator. God's creative work was not complete until He made woman.

God provided Adam a suitable partner (see Genesis 2:18) as he ruled the pure and undefiled world of creation. God didn't make another man; he made a woman. A woman is the *only* suitable partner for the man.

God designed Adam right from the beginning to be in charge, and in Eve he created someone to help and complement him. The man was called to be the leader, and the woman was called to be his partner. They were meant to be *equal in relationship and different in function.* The man's role is to protect, provide, preserve and care for the family.

When man marries, it's his responsibility to cling to his wife and to let go of his father and mother. He lets go of being cared for to embrace caring for others. The same responsibility his father had is now passed on to him. He no longer clings to his mother for her affections; he clings to his wife to give her what she needs. That's why a man leaves his father and mother and clings to his wife, and the

*The Role of the Man*

two of them become one body (see Genesis 2:24).

Bob's experience reflects the importance of leaving your father and mother when you marry. He married Sue, but he never stopped clinging to his mother. His mother was continually interfering and making decisions for Bob that he should have been making for himself and his wife. He would call her frequently, or she would call him, which continued an unhealthy dependence on her. Bob's marriage ended in divorce because of his unwillingness to cling to his wife instead of his mother.

## Distortion of the Male Role

God spoke to Adam and ordered him not to eat from the tree in the middle of the garden before Eve was created (see Genesis 2:15-18). Man's role is to listen to and obey God. So his role first became distorted when Adam chose to listen to and obey his wife instead of God, thus disobeying God's command.

Don and his bride moved into a new house less than a year after they were married. He had wanted to wait and save up some money first, but she had wanted a new home right away. Don was right to listen to her share her desires, but he wasn't listening to God's command to be the provider and protector of their marriage. She wanted new furnishings for their new home and insisted

*Secrets of a Happy Family*

on working to pay for them. He said nothing and watched her take over the control of their marriage.

The couple soon became parents. Despite the resulting expenses, Don said nothing when his wife bought a new car. He was like Adam, who had stood by and watched his wife make decisions that were not hers to make. And like Adam, Don also experienced disaster in his marriage. His lack of leadership cost them their home and finally their marriage.

Many men today listen to their wives' demands to buy expensive homes, clothes, cars and other luxuries. Men are being seduced into believing that wives feel more loved when their possessions far exceed what they need or can afford. They give in to their wives by working two jobs and allowing their wives to work outside the home in order to fulfill their wishes. Meanwhile, the children are being raised by a grandparent or even strangers so the parents can maintain a high material standard of living.

As Eve was being tempted by the serpent, Adam did nothing. As Eve was seduced by the serpent into eating from the restricted tree, Adam not only was unwilling to provide protection for her, but in fact disobeyed God's command in front of his wife. Adam's lack of spiritual leadership led his wife into sin.

Eve sinned because her husband Adam stood by her and did nothing to protect her from her act of disobedi-

*The Role of the Man*

ence. The woman saw that the tree was good for food, pleasing to the eyes and desirable for gaining wisdom. So she took some of its fruit and ate it; and she also gave some to her husband, *who was with her*, and he ate it (see Genesis 3:6). This *betrayal* of the woman by the man continues even today.

Tom's wife told him that their unmarried daughter was pregnant and needed an abortion so she could continue college. Tom knew it was against God's law, against Church teachings, but he didn't step in and say no to the abortion. He allowed his wife to take his daughter to have the abortion. Because of fear of conflict with his wife, his lack of spiritual leadership led his wife and daughter into serious sin.

Many women today faced with a pregnancy are seduced by Satan into getting an abortion while the father of the child stands by and does nothing to stop it. Any Christian should know God's commandment: "You shall not kill" Exodus 20:13). Yet just as Adam stood there and said nothing, fathers often do the same.

In the Garden of Eden, Adam started out in direct communication with God. God spoke to him directly when He commanded him not to eat from the tree of knowledge. Adam had listened to God and obeyed Him completely up until he went along with Eve's disobedience. At that point, however, Adam completely backed away from

*Secrets of a Happy Family*

his role as leader and protector. Though he *listened,* he did not *obey* what God told him in the very beginning.

## Rebellion

The Lord God then called to the man and asked him, "Where are you?" He answered, "I heard you in the garden; but I was afraid, because I was naked, so I hid myself." Then he asked, "Who told you that you were naked? You have eaten, then, from the tree of which I had forbidden you to eat!" The man replied, "The woman whom you put here with me—she gave me fruit from the tree, and so I ate it" (see Genesis 3:9-12).

Adam's decision to ignore God's command and *choose* to do something in opposition to God was tremendously destructive. When he *chose* to rebel against God's authority, he immediately forfeited his right of headship over the garden. Adam's rebellion was thus a complete abandonment of his headship over Eve. He failed to protect her from the serpent, who saw his failure to take his rightful role in stopping Eve from eating the forbidden fruit, and took the opportunity to seduce her. In fact, Adam caused not only Eve and himself, but all their descendants as well, to be attacked by sin, sickness and death.

Adam's refusal to obey God's command constituted a *rebellion.* A *rebellious* person does things his or her way instead of God's way. The rebellious person listens to no

*The Role of the Man*

one and doesn't obey lawful authority. The path of the rebellious person without repentance leads only to death, because the wages of sin are death (see Romans 6:23).

After the first couple's disobedience, to the man God said: "Because you listened to your wife and ate from the tree of which I had forbidden you to eat, cursed be the ground because of you! In toil shall you eat its yield all the days of your life. Thorns and thistles shall it bring forth to you, as you eat of the plants of the field. By the sweat of your face shall you get bread to eat, until you return to the ground, from which you were taken; for you are dirt, and to dirt you shall return" (Genesis 3:17-19).

Work was a joy before Adam sinned. God had provided everything. Whatever Adam did in caring for and cultivating the garden produced the best of crops. But after he sinned, no matter how hard he worked, he had to toil. Providing for his family became hard work; it came only by the sweat of his brow.

## Shifting blame

When Adam was confronted by God about why he was ashamed of his nakedness, he blamed his wife for the whole sad state of affairs, and she in turn blamed the serpent. Adam and Eve paid a high price—banishment from the garden—for his lack of spiritual leadership (see Genesis 3:23). The "Fall," as it came to be called, caused

*Secrets of a Happy Family*

Adam and Eve's curse to be passed on to all following generations.

Because of the Fall, man was to work by the sweat of his brow and woman was to experience pain in childbirth. Death would be the eventual outcome. When the sin of rebellion caused the Fall in the garden, Adam and Eve became subject to sin, sickness and death, along with all their descendants. Satan became the illegitimate landlord of the earth, "the god of the present age," as St. Paul called him (2 Corinthians 4:4).

Adam and Eve both shifted the blame for wrongdoing onto someone else. This attitude is the core of rebellion, and we see much of it in our society today.

Jim was a successful real estate agent and had a large family. He spent many hours at work and was away from home far too often. His wife told him many times that she was lonely and needed to talk to him.

She eventually became involved with another man because Jim wasn't there to give her quality time, time that included listening to her and giving her the attention that she was crying out for. Jim was devastated when his wife left him for the other man. He blamed her for the whole tragic situation.

Sadly, Jim never held himself accountable for not being with her when she needed him to be home. His frequent absences had contributed greatly to her sense of abandonment. He shifted the blame totally onto his wife and now he is alone, the marriage is ruined, and the children are victims of this divorce.

José was a legal alien residing in this country, a computer specialist married with four children. He knew that if he were convicted of a drug offense, the government could deport him. But he got involved in drugs anyway, and so he was deported from the United States.

José blamed the government for being racist because they were deporting him for drug convictions. He blamed his wife for reporting him to the police, and he blamed his lawyer for not trying hard enough to defend him because he was a poor legal alien. He never admitted that it was his own choice that caused his tragedy.

Because of José's choice to use drugs, his children will never see him again in this country. His story illustrates well how the refusal to accept responsibility for your own actions is the force that makes rebellion so destructive.

## Role reversal

In doing nothing to protect his wife, Adam was in great disobedience to God's command. Adam's lack of spiritual courage led his wife into sin. She took control of the situation and made the decision to disobey God's command. She took leadership that was not hers to take; this was in fact what today we call a *role reversal*.

*Secrets of a Happy Family*

Adam's betrayal of his role as the protector of Eve led her into making a decision on her own without the blessing of her husband and God. Eve knew that she was acting in disobedience to Adam, but she too chose to rebel against the lawful authority of God. She took away Adam's leadership and became the leader by her decision to disobey. She reversed roles by becoming the leader and making him the follower. Today, many men fail to be leaders in their families because their wife has accomplished a role reversal, and they're both allowing it to continue.

Another scriptural example of role reversal is found in the story of King Ahab of ancient Israel. Ahab wanted a certain piece of land with a vineyard. But the owner, whose name was Naboth, refused to sell it; it was his family inheritance.

Ahab knew that the law of the kingdom protected landowners from being forced to sell any inherited land, even if a king wanted it. Not able to get his way, Ahab came home angry and pouted like a child in the presence of his wife, Jezebel. He wouldn't eat and he grew sullen. In other words, he had a temper tantrum because he couldn't get what he wanted.

When Ahab told his wife what had upset him, she mocked him, wondering aloud what kind of king he was to be so weak. She told him not to worry and insisted that she would get the property for him. So he stood by and

## The Role of the Man

watched as she used deceit to have Naboth murdered and his property seized.

In this situation, Ahab led his wife into sin. He was just as responsible as Jezebel for the murder of Naboth.

A man named Tim provides a more contemporary example of role reversal. Tim is a passive and friendly guy. He's liked by everyone. His wife makes most of the decisions in their marriage.

In fact, Tim lets his wife assume responsibility for almost everything in their home. She single-handedly decided what type of careers her children were going to seek and where they were going to school. Tim just went along with the program.

Now the children are all raised and gone, and Tim and his wife live alone in a small house. His wife feels lost and lonely because she only has decisions to make for her sick husband. She took her husband's role of leadership many years ago, and now she's tired and wants to give it back to him.

But he doesn't want that role now. It's too late. She made a role reversal that's tearing them apart. And Tim's lack of spiritual leadership has now impacted several generations of his family.

Many marriages are in role reversal; this problem is one of the greatest causes of divorce today. Men aren't listening to God in providing and protecting their families against the evils in our society today. The kind of headship that leads men to raise their children spiritually and "bathe" their wives in the Word of God, making them holy, is almost unheard of (see Ephesians 5:26).

Spiritual, financial, emotional and sexual leadership is the man's responsibility. But in many cases he's relinquished this leadership to his wife so that she's had to take the full burden of it. Instead of delegating responsibility and being an overseer, he's given up his role to the woman.

Nevertheless, there's a "remnant" of those who still follow the biblical teachings of Jesus Christ—who are listening and obeying God. They are the strength of our nations today.

## Lack of male spirituality

We need to direct much of our prayer toward the male. The lack of male spirituality in our society has caused enormous damage. A major reason men don't know how to be men is that they lack spiritual role models.

We tend to equate true manliness with physical, emotional and financial power over others. We pay homage to athletes who make millions of dollars. We treat them as if they were gods. We buy the kind of shoes they wear, wash with the kind of soap they use. We buy the cars they like, and we drink the beer they advertise.

We try to imitate their sexual exploitation of women. Yes, we even use them, abuse them and then throw them

## The Role of the Man

aside. We tend to think that being rich or famous is the way to be a real man. In addition, our political life as a whole has often become as twisted as the character of some of our most deceitful politicians.

Satan is deceiving many men through the woman. Some men are still listening to the woman instead of God. They aren't taking the time to meditate and read His Word, and to listen to and obey the teachings of the Church. Their pride prevents them from having a spiritual director or submitting to an authority in the Church, one who has dedicated his life to proclaiming the gospel of Jesus Christ.

The need to pray for men is so critical that, unless men fall to their knees in repentance, the nations may very well be destroyed. Unwanted pregnancies would be stopped tomorrow if men accepted their responsibility of spiritual leadership. Males must also admit their responsibility for the international tragedy of abortion.

Men may play more than one immoral role in crimes of abortion. First, if the pregnancy has occurred outside of marriage, the male is a fornicator. The bottom line of responsibility for this situation is primarily his. Second, when an abortion takes place with the father's consent, then he is guilty of killing his own child, disobeying the fifth commandment: "Thou shall not kill." This sin is especially tragic because the biblical role of the male is to protect, not destroy.

*Secrets of a Happy Family*

Abortion is murder, an ugly act of ultimate violence against an innocent victim. Any male who has been an accomplice to an abortion needs to be reconciled with God and man before he can experience the presence of God in his life.

## Role Models

The only role model a man needs to follow is Jesus Christ. Jesus' whole mission was to do His Father's will, and men are called to do no less. In order for men to do the Father's will, they have to be formed by God's Word. If they become "men of the Word," their actions will then bring order to themselves, their families, their communities, their nation and, yes, even the whole world. To be a real man means to lead by serving others, just as Jesus led, served, died and loved us.

## Initiator

Men need to learn how to become accountable, to know when to act, and to know when to be silent. God's Word must be their manual. The Holy Spirit must be their Teacher.

A man is called to initiate, act, begin, make something happen. But men don't have the slightest idea what this means until they learn in Scripture what God in-

*The Role of the Man*

tends for them. A man is called to be a leader by following the lead of Christ. Christ's message to a man is, "Come follow me, and *die* to self."

"Husbands, love your wives, even as Christ loved the church and handed Himself over for her to sanctify her, cleansing her by the bath of water with the Word, that He might present to Himself the Church in splendor, without spot or wrinkle or any such thing, that she might be holy and without blemish" (Ephesians 5:25-27). As for the Christian, he's called upon to develop a new attitude of love, manifesting toward his wife a charity that's both gentle and strong like the gentle strength Christ shows the Church.

Men are called to love their wives just as Christ loved His bride (the Church, the people of God). Christ experienced ridicule, jeering, embarrassment, torture and finally even death for His bride. This is how a man must love his wife, by dying to himself for her. A man must suffer for his wife by putting her needs before his. He's called to protect her from all danger, such as ridicule from family or community.

The *Bread of Life Catholic Bible Study* asks: "How are husbands to act towards their wives?" The answer is found in Colossians 3:19: "Husbands, love your wives. Avoid any bitterness towards them."

The husband is to be his wife's encourager in anything

and everything. He is to die to his own ego by being a servant to her. When a man speaks in truth and gentleness, he cleanses her wounds caused by rejection from the world. He washes her clean with the message of hope found in the Sacred Scriptures. But a man can't do this if he doesn't know God's Word.

A man sanctifies his wife when the fruit of the Holy Spirit flows from him into her. The fruit of love, joy, peace, patience, kindness, gentleness, faithfulness, generosity and self-control (see Galatians 5:22-23) is what sanctifies and cleanses her. In this way he's leading her into the presence of God, bringing the couple both into harmony with God and with each other.

Men who love this way will seldom hear their wives complain of where they live or their lack of money. A woman will follow a man who loves her like this down the mouth of a cannon, and never look back.

## Obedience

We've heard it said that obedience is the core of love. Adam's disobedience caused death to all. St. Joseph (the foster father of Jesus) obeyed God by taking his family to Egypt (see Matthew 2:13-14). In doing so, he immediately saved the life of Jesus, who would later defeat death and make eternal life available to all who accepted Him.

Joseph was an ordinary man. He fell in love with and

## The Role of the Man

was engaged to Mary, who was pregnant by someone else, the Holy Spirit. Joseph was told by an angel from God in a dream that the Child was conceived by the Holy Spirit, and he was instructed to marry Mary and to name the Child Jesus (see Matthew 1:21). Joseph did all these things, showing how humble and obedient a man he was (see Matthew 1:20).

Joseph was a carpenter, a homebuilder a family man well known to the community. Yet in obedience to God, he responded to the angel's message immediately and took his wife and her Child off to the strange land of Egypt. It was a land that didn't recognize Joseph's faith or culture; it was a land of many pagan gods. Yet Joseph put his complete trust in God, and today we can marvel at his faith in and obedience to God's plan.

Joseph shows us a man who provided for and protected his family. He took his family and fled from Herod to Egypt. In accordance with custom, he spent a great deal of time teaching his foster Son a craft and spiritual knowledge. Joseph was a man of God, and he passed this great gift of faith on to Jesus. Proverbs 22:6 says: "Train a boy in the way he should go; even when he is old, he will not swerve from it." Joseph trained his child in the way he should go by being obedient to God. He recognized the voice of God, listened and obeyed.

Today, men are called to do no less than Joseph. Men

*Secrets of a Happy Family*

are called to give up the comfort of financial security if necessary to protect the values of the family. Men are called to protect their families against the evils of our society. Men are called, as Joseph was, to be the spiritual role model for their family.

Men need to learn that the more they die to their own needs, the more they're able to serve and meet the needs of others, especially their wives. A man is called to serve and protect, and he can't do that if he's still locked into himself. *The best way for men to get into and stay in God's presence is to get out of, and stay out of, their own presence.* Today, a man's role model as servant can be none other than the Suffering Servant, Christ. He was obedient even to death on the cross. He is a real Man; He is the Man we need to be like.

Nevertheless, when you declare that Jesus is the Lord and Master of your life, get ready, because persecution is on the way. The world doesn't consider Jesus Lord and Master of all. In fact, the world considers Jesus a worthless myth.

Men will always be persecuted for their belief in God and their obedience to Him. A man who refuses to be involved in fornication, for example, is often accused of not being a real man. Today, men who are faithful to their wives are many times laughed at by their fellows in the work place. But we must not worry about what the world says or does to us, because the Lord has promised us safety in the trial that's coming on the whole world (see Revelation 3:10).

## Responsibilities

"For the husband is head of his wife just as Christ is head of the church, He himself the Savior of the body" (Ephesians 5:23). The husband is responsible for the physical, emotional and spiritual health of his wife, just as Christ is responsible in these ways for the Church. The husband can't save his wife as Christ does, but he's responsible for leading her to Christ.

Communication needs to be operating fully between husband and wife if the role of the husband as a servant leader is to be established. A marriage, organization, or community without good lines of communication won't survive.

A husband's position as a leader in his marriage can be enhanced greatly when he's a man of his word. A man whose word is his bond is a man who will find a great deal of success in his marriage, organization and community.

## Servant Leader

What is servant leadership? "Jesus called them together and said to them: You know how among the Gentiles those who seem to exercise authority lord it over them; their great ones make their importance felt. It cannot be like that with you. Anyone among you who aspires to greatness must serve the rest; whoever wants to rank first among you must serve the needs of all. The Son of Man has not come to be served but to serve—to give His life in ransom for the many." (Mark 10:42-45).

The Holy Father reminds us: "Jesus as Christ exercises his royal power by serving us (see Mark 10:45); so also the Christian finds the authentic meaning of his participation in the kingship of his Lord in sharing His spirit and practice of service to man."[7]

A man is called to love his bride just as Christ loved *His* bride, which we call the Church. Christ loved His bride so much that He allowed Himself to suffer for her, to be tortured for her and even to be murdered for her. A man is called to do no less for his bride, and he does that every time he dies to his ego and to his own needs in order to meet her needs.

## Worship

To *worship* means to give reverence to Christ. It means to acknowledge and to recognize God. The focus of worship should be on God, not man. To worship truly, we must enter into God's presence and see Him face to face.

The way a man worships determines every facet of his

## The Role of the Man

life. He can only worship effectively when he's honest with God. God has to be at the center of his life. God has to be on the throne within his spirit. If he's not a man of worship, he'll find it difficult to maintain a healthy relationship with another person, nor can his marriage flourish.

Prayer is the core of all worship and the prelude to peace. As a man learns to put his trust in God, he becomes capable of trusting others, and he begins to discover the peace that surpasses all understanding (see Philippians 4:7). A man who worships God on a regular basis is a man who enters into the circle of power. God gives His grace to all who come to Him in humility and prayer.

The power of worship and praise has transformed millions of lives all around the world. Whoever sets his sights on becoming a man of prayer and worship soon becomes a man of strong, determined purpose as well. This path of humility, praise and prayer leads to the kind of worship that introduces a man into the presence of God Himself.

All a man's needs can be met while on his knees in prayer. It's in prayer and worship that we find that "God is among us" and is waiting to supply all our needs (see Philippians 4:19). "You husbands, too, must show consideration for those who share your lives. Treat women with respect as the weaker sex, heirs just as much as you to the gracious gift of life. If you do so, nothing will keep your prayers from being answered" (1 Peter 3:7).

## Questions for Reflection

- How does worship impact the quality of my life?
- How am I handling "role reversal"?
- How can I become more accountable to my spouse and others?

## Application of the Lesson

*Ephesians 5:25-26:* "Husbands, love your wives, as Christ loved the Church. He gave Himself up for her to make her holy, purifying her in the bath of water by the power of the word."

Husbands, each day this week, read a Scripture passage from the Gospel to your wife and talk about it.

Let us pray:

Lord, I desire to *listen* to whatever you tell me and to follow your lead in all I say and do. I ask you to close my ears to what is not from you and open my heart to your word and everlasting love. Amen

## CHAPTER THREE
# THE ROLE OF THE WOMAN
## Insights From Marie

"God created man in his image; in the Divine Image he created him; male and female he created them" (Genesis 1:27).

### Made in the Image of God (Love)

What does it mean to be made in the divine image of God? To be made in the divine image of God is to be made in love. The more that we become Christ-like in our actions, the clearer God's image will be seen in us.

We come to know God through His beloved Son, Jesus. What we have come to know of Jesus through His Word and the teachings of the Church is that He is all-loving, kind and merciful; slow to anger, full of compassion and forgiving of wrongdoing. Throughout the New Testament we see how Jesus lived, how He acted, how He healed, and how He revealed the great love of the Father for each one of us.

*Secrets of a Happy Family*

## Basic need for love

We're told in 1 John 4:8 that God is love. To love, and to be loved, is the basic need of every human being.

So what has happened to the child who was created in the image and likeness of God—to love and be loved? That image of God becomes distorted by sin.

Of course, we could blame our ancestors or other circumstances all the way back to Eve for the way we are today. That way we wouldn't have to take responsibility for our own actions. Many of us have in fact done this for years—but we're only shunning responsibility for our own behavior when we do.

Many things in our lives tend to pervert our understanding of love and how wives are to love their husbands. Perhaps one of the biggest offenders that so easily leads us to sin is the entertainment media, particularly TV. Through TV, we learn the world's distorted way of life—not God's true way. The following testimony illustrates this point.

## Distortion of love

I used to watch soap operas on TV in our first years of marriage and became terribly disillusioned when I started comparing my relationship with Ken to the relationships on the screen. By this standard I tried to evaluate the extent to

## The Role of the Woman

which he was loving me or failing to love me. Tremendous tension in our marriage resulted because I placed expectations on Ken to love me according to the world's distorted view of love.

The world places the emphasis on self and self-fulfillment; God's way is just the opposite. In truth, love is the emptying of yourself, the desire to meet the other's need through self-sacrifice. "Such is the case with the Son of Man who has come not to be served by others but to serve, to give His own life as a ransom for the many" (Matthew 20:28).

I blamed Ken and my parents for a lack of understanding and love until the day when the Lord opened my eyes. Like the blind man Jesus healed, I came to see my own sinfulness. I had spent years looking for love from other people, not realizing that the fulfilling love of God was already there; I had only to look to Him, not to others. As I looked to God and came to Him, He filled me with His unconditional love.

Before, I'd expected to receive this unconditional love from man; in fact, I'd demanded it. Then, when I hadn't received it, I'd blamed my husband for not loving me. In reality, however, only God could fill that need to be loved unconditionally.

I had put my whole trust in my husband, yet hadn't received unconditional love in return. So I'd become angry, bitter, resentful and unforgiving toward him. The result was depression.

*Secrets of a Happy Family*

No matter how hard my husband had tried to love me, I would find fault. I was looking for God and expecting man to give me what only God could give me. Jeremiah 17:5 describes what I was doing for years. "Cursed is the man who trusts in human beings, who seeks his strength in human beings, who seeks his strength in flesh, whose heart turns away from the Lord."

When I began to trust in God completely rather than in man, my life took a big turn. We experience God's love working through man when we stop looking at man's faults and look with the eyes of God.

During the time when I was resentful toward Ken, I would spend much time in prayer and reading Scripture in the early morning hours. Whenever Ken asked me questions, I became irritated with him for interrupting my time with God. Of course, I was just fooling myself in thinking that God was pleased with my sacrifice of time with Him when at the same time I clung to a bad attitude toward my husband.

"Your attitude must be that of Christ" (Philippians 2:5). "If anyone says, I love God, yet hates his brother, he is a liar. For anyone who does not love his brother, whom he has seen, cannot love God, whom he has not seen" (1 John 4:20).

Scripture says that this kind of behavior is a kind of lie. And who is the author of lies? Yes, Satan. He is both a deceiver and a liar.

Just as he did with Eve, he goes after the woman to get

to the man. He attacks through her emotions. Irritation and anger often follow, and when she gives in to the temptation, she drags the man into sin. Her irritation many times causes her spouse to withdraw, become defensive, turn off and tune her out. On the other hand, Scripture tells us that the hidden character of the heart expressed in the unfading beauty of a calm and gentle disposition is precious in God's eyes (see 1 Peter 3:4). This is what turns a man on.

## True meaning of love

The role of the woman is to be an affirmer, an encourager and a partner made in the divine image of God. She is one who's always to be there for her husband because, as Scripture says, it's not good for man to be alone (see Genesis 2:18).

A human being is the only creature on earth with the incredible gift of a soul with a free will. A woman can choose life or death with each choice that she makes. When she encourages or affirms or is there for her husband, she chooses life, and this choice is another step for her in her journey to become Christ-like.

A woman is equal in her relationship to a man in the eyes of God. She is called to be one who completes man, not one who competes with him. She enhances all that's noble about him and she empowers him to be the servant leader God has chosen him to be.

*Secrets of a Happy Family*

A woman, being a responder, becomes accustomed to expressing a sacrificial love. She gives of her love completely. By nature most women are nurturers; that is, they extend love through compassion, healing, mercy, forgiveness and affirmation.

A woman's nurturing spirit is fragile, and yet because of its depth, it's enormously powerful. A woman who knows who she is because she knows that God loves her and has taken away her sins is capable of expressing love. "Love consists in this: not that we have loved God, but that He has loved us and has sent His Son as an offering for our sins" (1 John 4:10).

## Made as Co-Creator

God blessed Adam and Eve, saying: "Be fertile and multiply; fill the earth and subdue it. Have dominion over the fish of the sea, the birds of the air, and all the living things that move on the earth" (Genesis 1:28). A woman's role, according to these verses, is to give birth, fill the earth and subdue it along with her husband.

Ken and I were married for four years before we learned there was a strong possibility that we wouldn't be able to have children. This was traumatic for both of us. The emotional strain of surgery, counting days, and much time and money spent on doctors caused tension in our sexual relationship.

## The Role of the Woman

We finally decided to adopt. We discovered that the emotional preparation involved in adopting a child is much like the nine months of pregnancy. The anticipation builds and excitement grows as the time approaches.

After we adopted, I seldom thought about not being able to conceive and bear a child. But later in life, I suddenly sensed a loss that I had never known was there. I read in the Bible that having a child is what gives meaning to a woman (see Genesis 30:23). The thought that I would never experience having a child began disturbing me again.

This feeling went on for quite a while until I heard a certain woman speaking on Mary, the mother of God. Suddenly I experienced in my womb a filling of His Holy Spirit. At that time, God revealed to me that I would give birth in a different way.

I experienced, through the Holy Spirit, a birth of the Word of God to be shared with many people in the Church. I felt fulfilled knowing that God would use me in a special, nurturing way. Today, I can humbly see all the spiritual children who have come into being through my teaching the Word of God.

The Lord blessed me further when my oldest daughter invited me into the delivery room to experience the birth of our first grandson. Actually to witness God's creation, a child, come into this world is indeed to behold a miracle. I truly did experience the miracle of giving birth that day. When

*Secrets of a Happy Family*

you love the Lord, eye cannot see, ear cannot hear, what God has in store for you (see 1 Corinthians 2:9).

## Made as Partner
## Integral part of man

Today, Ken and I are still open to conceiving, though I'm past the child-bearing age. We know that all things are possible with the Lord. Sarah laughed at the thought of having a child, yet she did conceive in her old age and bore a son. We laugh when we think about the possibility and even hope it may happen. We now pray before intercourse and are open to God's will for us.

"The Lord God said: 'it is not good for the man to be alone. I will make a suitable partner for him'" (Genesis 2:18). God's purpose in bringing woman into being was to fill man's loneliness and provide a suitable partner for him. The Lord cast a deep sleep on the man, and while he was sleeping, He took out one of Adam's ribs and closed up its place with flesh. Then the Lord God made a woman from the rib he had taken out of the man, and he brought her to the man.

"In creating the human race 'male and female,'" says Pope John Paul II, "God gives man and woman an equal personal dignity, endowing them with the inalienable rights and responsibilities proper to the human person."[8] When the woman was brought to the man, the man said,

## The Role of the Woman

"This one, at last, is bone of my bones and flesh of my flesh; this one shall be called 'woman,' for out of 'her man' this one has been taken" (Genesis 2:23). If woman was taken out of man, then she is not complete without him. And because she's a part of him, he's not complete without her. Of course, God calls some people to a celibate life, and when He does, He gives them graces to make them complete even without a spouse. But in general, because man and woman were made for each other, they are incomplete without each other.

The role of a woman (part of man) is thus to love her husband by meeting his needs. His role is to love her as he loves himself, because she is part of him. We're to be united and become one flesh. God calls for man and woman to reserve sexual union for the sacred bond of marriage only.

At the resurrection of Jesus, an angel of the Lord appeared to Mary Magdalene and the other Mary. The angel told them that Jesus, the Crucified, had been raised from the dead. The angel also said not to be afraid, but rather to go quickly to tell His disciples He had been raised, where He was going, and that they would see Him there. As the women were going, Jesus appeared to them and said, "Do not be afraid. Go and carry the news to my brothers that they are to go to Galilee, where they will see me" (Matthew 28:10).

*Secrets of a Happy Family*

The women's role in this episode was that of messengers. Women need to be reassured at times by God and told how to deal with the situations in their lives. We must listen to God and follow what He tells us to do in Scripture. Then we can act as messengers to our spouses, sharing what God tells us.

A woman recently asked me if Ken would encourage her husband to attend a Benedictus Breakfast, a ministry of men ministering to men. I told him about her request, and then one morning, in my prayer time, this incident came back to mind. The Holy Spirit put it on my mind that women are to encourage their husbands by sharing with them whatever the Lord reveals to them.

He often tells us in our prayer times, during the day, while doing our chores—in fact, anytime—where we can find Jesus. Just as Jesus gave the instructions to the women to tell the men where to find Him, He's telling you and me over and over not to be afraid. Don't be afraid to tell the men in your life where they can find Jesus.

The Holy Father confirms this insight: "The sensitive respect of Jesus toward the women that He called to his following and His friendship, His appearing on Easter morning to a woman before the other disciples, the mission entrusted to women to carry the good news of the resurrection to the apostles—these are all signs that confirm the special esteem of the Lord Jesus for women."[9]

*The Role of the Woman*

Women, share with the men in your life all the times the Lord comes to you and all the things He says to you. Share the love relationship you have with Jesus. Don't be afraid, even if you've been rejected before.

If they are disobedient to God or caught up in the world, it may take a while. Meanwhile, you're called to obey God in whatever He tells you. Do what you're told, and let God take care of the men in your life. Imitate the obedience of Mary Magdalene when God told her to tell the disciples where to go to find Jesus.

## Responds to man

Women are responders by nature. They respond positively or negatively, often depending on whether they're in role reversal. If they're responding to the man as leader and initiator, they respond positively. If they themselves are leading and initiating, their response is negative, as was Eve's in the garden. She initiated role reversal by eating the fruit and giving it to her husband.

"God then manifests the dignity of women in the highest form possible," the Holy Father notes, "by assuming human flesh from the Virgin Mary, whom the church honors as the mother of God, calling her the new Eve and presenting her as the model of redeemed woman."[10] Mary, the mother of Jesus, always responded positively because she followed the lead of God and her husband. Mary is

*Secrets of a Happy Family*

truly the humble handmaid of the Lord.

Humility is the key to love and loving relationships. In the *Bread of Life Catholic Bible Study* we ask: "What has the Lord looked upon and what would all ages call Mary?" (see Luke 1:48). We're told in the Scripture that He looked upon the humble state of His servant, and that all ages would call her blessed.

As a woman, Mary is the perfect role model. Her response to the angel was simple: "I am the servant of the Lord. Let it be done to me as you say" (Luke 1:38). She responded to God's message in faith by visiting her kinswoman, Elizabeth. She responded to the angel by yielding herself to God's will for her life.

God has a plan for us, different for each one. The best way to know that plan is to yield ourselves to Him. How do we yield? By listening and obeying Him.

Mary became pregnant when the Holy Spirit came upon her and the power of the Most High overshadowed her (see Luke 1:35). Her response to God's initiative was this: "I am the servant of the Lord. Let it be done to me as you say."

Mary had a free will and could have objected. But she chose to yield her body to her spouse, the Holy Spirit. Do we yield our bodies to our spouses?

When she visited her kinswoman Elizabeth, Mary responded to Elizabeth's greeting by praising God for what

## The Role of the Woman

He had done for her. Mary talks about the greatness of the Lord and how her spirit finds joy in her Savior. In Mary's canticle, she refers twelve times to all God has done for her, and her praises ring throughout these verses (see Luke 1:46-55).

There are few words of Mary in the Bible, but those few point in a tremendously important direction for women today. Humility is a strong characteristic of Mary, openness to let God do what He wants with her. She is trusting, humble, submissive, obedient; her spirit rejoices in God her Savior. She is a perfect role model for all women.

Mary responded to Joseph in quiet submission by traveling with him to register for the census as ordered by Caesar Augustus. She didn't rely on feelings. She probably wasn't feeling well, being ready to give birth. Yet Mary responded to Joseph and followed his lead. He was the initiator, and she responded to him. Her humility is a prime example of real submission.

Mary responded to the shepherds by pondering what they said about the Savior in her heart. She responded to the angel and her husband in naming the Child Jesus. She marveled about what was said about her Son. When Jesus was found in the temple after being lost for three days, she responded by asking Him why He didn't tell them where He was. Although she didn't understand, she treasured all these things in her heart.

*Secrets of a Happy Family*

At the wedding feast Mary responded to Jesus by instructing the servants to do whatever He told them. She responded to John when Jesus, from the cross, gave her to him (see John 19:27). Mary responded by being part of community. Acts 1:14 says, "They all joined together constantly in prayer, along with the women, and Mary the mother of Jesus, and his brethren." She responded to God in prayer and praise to Him.

## Submission to man

"Wives should be submissive to their husbands as to the Lord" (Ephesians 5:22). Submission is an often misused word. It doesn't mean becoming a doormat. Jesus, at whose name every knee shall bow in heaven and on earth (see Philippians 2:10), submitted His will to His Father, and we honor Christ by following His example.

We see from St. Paul's words to the Ephesians that a wife is called to be submissive to her husband. This form of submission is certainly not limited to the woman, according to Ephesians 5:21, which says, "Defer to one another out of reverence for Christ." Both man and woman are being called to be submissive to one another out of reverence for Christ, which means loving one another as we love Christ. That's why it's so important to have a personal relationship with Christ.

Submission doesn't mean to obey; in the family, only

## The Role of the Woman

children are called upon to obey, and they must obey their parents (see Ephesians 6:1). A wife is not a child awaiting orders to "Do this! Get that! Fix me that! Get my lunch!" She isn't a child, nor is she a slave.

When I married, I went into my new relationship totally dependent on my husband in everything. I did everything he told me and felt secure in the relationship with him until he had to have major lung surgery, five years after we were married. Our baby girl was ten months old, and the circumstances surrounding the surgery forced me to take a job outside the home to help support our little family. We were living with my mother and father at the time.

I began to feel insecure and unloved. Smoking and eating became my comforts. Ken was preoccupied with his illness, and the baby and job were taking so much of my time that it seemed I was getting short-changed in the love department.

When my husband finally went back to work after many months, I stayed home with our baby. Ken was so thankful that the Lord let him live that he became deeply involved with church activities. I grew more and more withdrawn and distant from him.

I thought I was being submissive because I continued to do what was asked of me, but inside I was a time bomb ready to explode. All I did was care for the home

*Secrets of a Happy Family*

and children (by this time we had three adopted children) and wait on Ken. I tried, though unsuccessfully, to keep myself slim because he didn't like me to put on weight.

Each day when he arrived home from work, Ken would ask me whether I'd done my exercises that day. I was compulsively eating and gaining weight. I loved to cook, and I tried out everything to see how it tasted. I ate whatever others left because I didn't want to waste anything. I would even sneak food when Ken wasn't around. At the same time, I smoked about two packs of cigarettes a day, yet I still felt unfulfilled.

I was trying to please my husband, but I kept failing and became more and more compulsive, looking for love in food. My understanding of submission was totally distorted. I was inwardly rebelling against my husband.

Much of what a wife does in silence may give the appearance of being in submission while, in reality, it's nothing less than capitulation. Submission is the act of giving oneself totally in the presence of love; capitulation is giving oneself totally in the presence of fear. A prison inmate, for example, will quickly, quietly and in an orderly manner do what he's told. Yet inside, he's in rage or rebellion.

We also must not think that to be submissive is to be inferior. On the contrary, it's a God-ordained distinction

## The Role of the Woman

in function, intended to preserve our society. We must always be aware that, for the sake of unity within the marriage relationship, a woman is to be subject to the leadership of her husband.

She's not a slave, but she is one who's provided for, cared for and secured by her husband (see Genesis 3:16). When she feels this caring from her husband, submission in a relationship between a husband and wife is intimate. In submission a wife absolutely, joyfully and willingly responds to her husband in anything but *sin* (see Ephesians 5:22). Where sin is involved, she is of course to obey God and not man (see Acts 5:29).

*What a wife does for her husband is not nearly as important as how much love there is in her action.* We need only look to Scripture to see that before sin entered the world, the wife lovingly submitted to her husband's care, protection and leadership, where *the husband lovingly and sacrificially gave himself* to meet every need of his wife. If we are to see and experience that kind of relationship in our marriages today, we must be filled with the Spirit (see Ephesians 5:18). Being Spirit-filled makes it possible for a wife to submit to her husband and for a husband to love his wife.

Submission is *willingly* putting aside your self-interests to care for the needs of the other. Philippians 2:3-4 tells us: "Do nothing out of selfishness or out of vainglory; rather, humbly regard others as more important

*Secrets of a Happy Family*

than yourselves, each of you looking to others' interest, rather than to his own."

To submit is closely related to humbling yourself. It means not thinking of your own wants and needs, but thinking of the other person's interests, thinking of what's best for that person.

Woman submits to man because man, who was created first, is to have authority over his wife. For Adam was formed first, then Eve. Further, Adam was not deceived, but the woman was deceived and transgressed (see 1 Timothy 2:11-14). The wife was made out of his body (see Genesis 2:21-24) to be his helper and companion (see Genesis 2:20). She is to honor her husband by submitting to him as her head (see 1 Corinthians 11:3).

Consider these two examples of a wife's submission:
- To encourage her husband, who has a terrible arthritic condition in his back and spine, a wife may *choose* many times to be the driver of the car, even though she dislikes driving and is tired.
- Sometimes a wife can tell when her husband wants to make love, and she *chooses* to go beyond her feelings of tiredness or a bad mood, encouraging him to make love to her. Many times after they make love, she feels so much better and her whole mood changes.

*The Role of the Woman*

In both examples the key words are *choose* and *encourage*. She chose and encouraged when she willingly gave of herself.

## Free will

God has given us a free will with which we can choose to follow Him or to reject Him. This free will is at the heart of love. He created us but didn't force us to love Him. He gave us the freedom to choose life or death.

Freedom comes when we choose to follow Him. Slavery comes when we choose to follow Satan and the way of the world. Our battle is not against flesh and blood, but against principalities and powers through which Satan rules the earth until Jesus comes again (see 2 Corinthians 4:4).

Satan was thrown out of heaven and prowls around seeking anyone he can devour. But Jesus defeated Satan on the cross. When we choose to make Jesus Lord of our life and follow His way through obedience to His Word, then we're on the road to living the abundant life.

Some of us open doors to let Satan gain a foothold. Our freedom to choose can result in our being held in bondage to sin. It's usually in some area of weakness—food, sex, alcohol or some other temptation.

For instance, Jane's weak area is overeating. God healed Jane quite a few years ago of compulsive eating, but she's still tempted at times. She had an incident recently in which she had to tell herself and Satan out loud that she was going to choose life over death (see Deuteronomy 30:19). She came to recognize that she opens doors for Satan to come in and tempt her to sin through food, her weak area.

Jane's healing came through the Scripture when she read: "For there is One greater in you than there is in the world" (1 John 4:4). The realization of what Jesus did on the cross, His death and resurrection, came to her. It took on new meaning to say that by taking all her sins on Himself, Jesus defeated Satan's hold on her.

When the Lord ascended into heaven and sent her His Holy Spirit, He gave her the strength to choose to eat small amounts of food. He will never come in and take away the freedom to choose. If He did, the relationship would be a dictatorship, not love. But He gives her the grace to choose obedience.

Jane acknowledged the Holy Spirit's presence within her and Jesus' defeat of Satan who was tempting her. Whenever she called on God and recognized His presence, she had self-control, a fruit of the Holy Spirit.

Jane had to understand that eating more than she needed to function, and eating unhealthy foods that can cause bodily harm, was *sin*. She tried many ways over the years to excuse her sin of gluttony, even though the Church has long considered it one of the seven cardinal sins. She

*The Role of the Woman*

used every excuse in the book to continue to choose to overindulge.

Her excuses ran the gamut: "This isn't really sin." "God doesn't care about what I eat." "I've got to make sure my family is well fed and everyone has enough to eat." "If I didn't have to cook, I wouldn't eat so much." "I can't waste this food when there are starving children out there."

She even blamed her husband for her overeating, using the excuse, "I don't feel loved." (Love, of course, is not a feeling; it's a decision. She had a wrong understanding of love.) All these excuses gave Satan a foothold.

God's grace has now given Jane the ability to say no to Satan. She recently made the choice of saying no, for example, after missing breakfast at a convention. Arriving home, she found leftovers for both her husband and herself. Her husband chose to eat cereal instead; but she, feeling starved, reheated the double portion, plus bread.

Although she prayed to the Holy Spirit not to overeat, she nevertheless explained to her husband that eating two portions was not overeating because she'd had no breakfast. This explanation, she eventually came to believe, came from the voice of Satan. Fortunately, the Holy Spirit also spoke, and she *chose* to obey His direction. She put back the excess leftovers and felt she was a conqueror through Jesus Christ.

Jane didn't want to block God's grace from flowing through her, especially because she and her husband were preparing to give a talk on the family. She knew that she can do all things through Christ who strengthens her. She is more and more aware of His presence within her. Yielding to Him, she feels much better about herself. Feeling good about herself and taking responsibility for her actions, she doesn't blame others.

An important aspect of the first sin in Eden was displayed when Adam blamed Eve, and Eve blamed the serpent. They weren't taking responsibility for their actions. But God has given His Holy Spirit to strengthen us, to empower us, to choose life over death.

Jane praises and thanks God for the victory. He was pleased with Solomon for asking for wisdom and understanding. He is pleased when we choose to yield to his Spirit within us. He can then use our temples of His Spirit to reach out to a lost, hurting world.

## Role Reversal

"I will intensify the pangs of your childbearing; in pain shall you bring forth children. Yet your *urge* shall be for your husband, and he shall be your master" (Genesis 3:16, emphasis added). The urge a woman has for a man is to have him

*The Role of the Woman*

love her, protect her, take care of her, even lead her to Jesus. Women have a need for men to be the physical, emotional and spiritual heads that they are called to be.

Before the fall, Adam loved Eve in the same way that Christ loves the Church. In women who are in role reversal and taking the headship that belongs to the man, their *urge* is to control the man, to get him to eat the fruit just as Eve did with Adam. She wants to fill *her own appetite* and get her husband to agree with her choice.

In the genuine line of authority, the male's authority comes from Christ. The woman's authority comes from the man. The child's authority comes from the parents.

Because of the fall, however, the man believes his authority comes from himself. But he's in the wrong when he does, and his authority is ineffectual. He becomes her "master"—that is, he treats her like a slave, controlling dominating and oppressing her.

When a man claims his authority comes from himself, not from God, he no longer listens to and obeys God. But when man listens to and obeys God, woman responds. Both enjoy unity in the marriage.

*Secrets of a Happy Family*

## Questions for Reflection

- How do I complement my spouse?
- How can I be subject to authority or to my husband as to the Lord?
- In what way have I submitted to God and others?

## Application of the Lesson

*Ephesians 5:22:* "Wives should be submissive to their husbands as if to the Lord."

Show how you have submitted to your husband as you would to God. Submit to your husband as if he were Christ. Daily tell your husband how you see Christ in him.

Let us pray:

Lord, show us how to be the man or woman you have called us to be. You are truly our Lord and Master. We will follow You by following those You have placed in authority over us. We love You, Lord, and desire to do Your will. Amen

## CHAPTER FOUR
# THE ROLE OF THE COUPLE
## In God's Divine Image

In two biblical passages—one from the Old Testament, and one from the New—we find the essentials laid out for the role of the married couple: They are created in the divine image, and their relationship is centered in Christ.

"God created man in His image, in the divine image He created him; male and female He created them. *God blessed them*, saying: 'Be fertile and multiply; fill the earth and subdue it. Have dominion over the fish of the sea, the birds of the air, and all the living things that move on the earth.' God also said: 'See, I give you every seed-bearing plant all over the earth and every tree that has seed-bearing fruit on it to be your food; and to all the animals of the land, all the birds of the air, and all the living creatures that crawl on the ground, I give all the green plants for food.' And so it happened. God looked at everything He had made, and He found it *very good*. Evening came, and morning followed—the sixth day" (Genesis 1:27-31, emphasis added).

"I want you to know that the head of every man is Christ; the head of the woman is her husband; and the head of

Christ is the Father" (1 Corinthians 11:3).

The role of the married couple is to become Christ-like, and the love between them is to be identified with the love relationship Christ has with the Church (that is, with us). They are to be co-creators in bringing new life into the world. The couple is to be united as one in following Christ's lead by listening and obeying Him. The husband and wife are to complement one another.

## Role

In the beginning of the book of Genesis, God tells us He created man, not just in His image, but His *divine* image. God created the male first, then He created the female. He made them both in the image of Himself. This means that God is Spirit, and they had attributes of God's Spirit within them.

The human being is the only earthly creature born with a soul that has a free will. This free will allows man to choose life or death—that is, good or evil. An animal isn't capable of making intellectual choices.

Every time man chooses to love, he becomes more Christ-like. As he continues to love, he reflects more clearly God's own divine image. Man's journey through the kingdom of God is a process of becoming more and more a divine image of God. In our society today, man and woman are equal in relationship to God, but their

*The Role of the Couple*

function is different. This difference is noted in the very beginning of the Sacred Scriptures.

## Function

Adam's main function was to initiate, provide and protect. He was to plan, execute, act and *love*. Eve's main function, on the other hand, was to affirm, console, serve and *respect*. As a couple, Adam and Eve were told to be fertile and multiply. The very first command God gave them was to have intercourse and bear children.

## Equality of Relationship

God looked on Adam and Eve as equals; neither one was better, higher or more important than the other. The "woman"—as we've noted, the word means "out of man"—was made to complete Adam. They were equal because they were both made in the image of God. The difference between them was in their function.

This insight is verified in several scriptural texts. "There does not exist among you Jew or Greek, slave or freeman, male or female. All are one in Christ Jesus" (Galatians 3:28). This passage tells us that we are all equal in God's eyes. The relationship that God has with His children is based on love, not on gender. That's why today women are taking more roles of authority and responsibility in the development of the Church.

*Secrets of a Happy Family*

"All of you who have been baptized into Christ have clothed yourselves with him" (Galatians 3:27). The *Bread of Life Catholic Bible Study* asks the question: "With what five things are we to clothe ourselves, and for what reason"? The answer appears in Colossians 3:12: "Because you are God's chosen ones, holy and beloved, clothe yourselves with heartfelt mercy, with kindness, humility, meekness and patience."

When the man and woman clothe themselves with Christ, they then allow God's Spirit to flow through them and complement one another, thus becoming one heart and mind. Unity comes when both man and woman are following Christ and doing things His way—not their own way.

## Sexual Activity
## God's Blessing

God gave us the beautiful and life-giving gift of sex. Sex is to be shared, developed and enjoyed only by a husband and his wife. The husband is called to protect her, provide for her and love her.

God never said, "Be fruitful and multiply unless it becomes inconvenient for you." He never said, "Multiply and be fruitful unless it interferes with your career." He never said, "Just have sex without being open to multiplying."

God clearly mandates that the call to be fruitful and multiply can only be between a man and a woman; there-

*The Role of the Couple*

fore, a "marriage" between two people of the same sex cannot fulfill God's command. "You shall not lie with a male as with a woman; such a thing is an abomination" (Leviticus 18:22). God Himself gave man His highest form of vocation when He told him to go forth and be, with his wife, a co-creator—a co-creator of human life, a miracle above all other miracles.

## Natural Family Planning (NFP)

The method called Natural Family Planning (NFP) allows couples to space their children without using contraception. An NFP couple, through abstinence during specific times of the fertile cycle, does nothing to interrupt the actual act of creation. The husband and wife learn respect for each other during fertile times, and they both are part of the planning.

This method requires responsibility on the part of both partners. It calls for obedience to God and discipline. In other words, it's not a guy thing or a girl thing; it's planning a family naturally by both husband and wife.

## Contraception

God's first command to Adam and Eve was to be fertile, fill the earth and subdue it. "Thus the fundamental task of the family," says Pope John Paul II, "is to serve life, to actualize in history the original blessing of the creator—that of transmitting by procreation the divine image from person to person."[11]

Unfortunately, many men and women have decided that to multiply in the sexual union of marriage is not a blessing from God. No wonder there is so much pain and needless suffering in the world today! Couples have decided to take matters into their own hands, rejecting God's blessing by practicing birth control using artificial means.

Contraception means being separated. Those couples who decide to use contraception are separating themselves from God's basic call to Adam and Eve to be fertile and multiply (Genesis 1:28). When we remove the decision to trust Him, we replace it with the decision to rebel, and we simply become our own god.

In the practice of artificial birth control, we ourselves decide who will exist and who will not exist. The term "artificial" means the interruption of the process that leads to creation, by such means as an IUD (intrauterine device), condom, pill, RU 486, spermicide or sterilization. These are all artificial ways of preventing a pregnancy, and some are actually forms of abortion.

Contraception is a violation of the intention of God's gift of sexual intercourse—that the possibility of life always be present. Some couples unintentionally allow a new life to come into existence, then decide to end this life. In other words, they murder a child through abortion.

*The Role of the Couple*

Through both contraception and abortion, we've deviated greatly from the divine command to go forth, be fertile and multiply. We've learned painfully that the road of rebellion leads from contraception to abortion and now to euthanasia. We now have completed the cycle of death as we rush to judgment day.

When a husband has sex with his wife and tries to avoid the first divine command given to a married couple, "Be fertile and multiply" (Genesis 1:28), he is in *sin*. Men have become seduced into thinking that these are different times and the rules have changed. But God's call to be His co-creators hasn't changed. He wants our love and desire for each other to lead to the beauty of creation.

God never advised a husband to use his wife as a plaything. He never told man to use, abuse and then throw her away like a dirty disposable cup. He told the man that he was to love his bride just as Christ loved His bride—that is, as He loved us, the Church.

Christ cherished His bride; He suffered for her; He was tortured for her; He allowed Himself to be murdered for her. But in contrast to this genuine, self-sacrificing love, many men practice a distorted kind of love. Instead of loving people and using things, they love things and use people. And this distortion of love has been passed

*Secrets of a Happy Family*

down throughout the ages.

Some may snicker at this simple viewpoint of life and of God's holy Word. They may scoff at the notion that God should be in complete control of our lives. But they pay a steep price for rejecting His authority.

Sin certainly has entered our world through contraception, which is only one way in which we reject God's blessing of the gift of sexuality. That rejection takes other forms as well: rape; incest; and abortion, which is a crime against the fifth commandment, "Thou shall not kill." All these grow from selfishness, lawlessness and greed. And they have a single remedy: *obedience to God's Word.*

## Abortion

How can a nation be seriously concerned about air pollution, housing, jobs and peace—yet be killing their children in the wombs of their own mothers? Although a ghetto or war zone is a dangerous place for a child to live today, in any cases the most dangerous place for an unwanted child is in his mother's womb. Scripture tells us that to stand by and watch these children being murdered through abortion while doing nothing to stop the killing is more than dishonorable; it's evil (see Proverbs 24:11).

A young woman had an abortion over five years ago when she was twenty years old. She couldn't believe that she had gotten herself into such a situation, alone, preg-

## The Role of the Couple

nant and so young. So she had her baby aborted.

By her own account, her desperation and loneliness became ten times worse after the abortion. She turned to alcohol. She drank heavily for several months until she hit rock bottom and tried to kill herself six months after the abortion.

All she felt in her life at that time was pain—a pain so deep that not even alcohol could numb it. She wanted to be with her aborted baby so badly that she thought by killing herself they would be together forever. She just wanted her baby back, even if it meant dying to be with him.

Nevertheless, this young woman was blessed with close friends who reminded her of how much God loved her. Today she knows that if it weren't for their care and concern for her, she probably would have committed suicide.

Years went by, and she learned to cope with her guilt and grief alone. She survived her abortion experience, but she still felt far apart from the Lord. Why? Because of this great sin she had committed: the murder of her own child. She didn't feel worthy of love from anyone—especially from God.

One weekend she attended a healing workshop offered at her church. Her whole life changed. For the first time since her abortion, she felt loved and forgiven by the Lord.

She asked the Lord for forgiveness for everything she had done and knew at that moment of confession that the

Lord, her Father, forgave her. His mercy was overpowering. Through the people at the workshop she was shown how God forgives her and loves her.

Afterward she began attending a Bible study, where she discovered an even deeper knowledge of the Lord and His great mercy. Through a Holy Spirit Seminar and the *Bread of Life Catholic Bible Study* she has received more inspiration, and now she has a passion to know the Lord and to seek Him always in all she does. She thanks all those who have been her "light" in her time of darkness.

She still thinks about her child, of course, and grieves for him. She'll always have a special place in her heart for him. But she knows now that the Lord has a special plan for her. She believes that God will fill her with courage and strength to go on with life.

## Obedience

We must return to obeying God by loving one another the way Christ has loved us. Sex is one of the most powerful gifts that God has given us. God always intended it to be a life-giving gift of intimacy and pleasure. God has given a husband and wife the chance to express their deepest emotions about each other and Him through sexual lovemaking. When a husband and wife love each other in the way God has called them to love, according to His holy Word, they catch a glimpse of the intimacy of heaven.

*The Role of the Couple*

God's Word has dramatically changed our lives and our marriage. In God's holy Word Ken has learned how to love his wife sexually, emotionally and spiritually. God has shown Ken in His Word that he must never defile the marriage bed.

Being a man of the Word, Ken is now much more aware of Marie's yearning for his sexual, emotional and spiritual leadership. God has shown him in His Word that he's called to be the *initiator* in the sexual, emotional and spiritual development of their relationship. That leadership takes place as long as he's obedient to God's holy Word. When Ken submits to his wife as he submits to Christ, then Christ will honor his obedience all the days of his life.

A scriptural example of being obedient to the Word in this regard is shown in the book of Tobit. This book includes a powerful story of a young man, Tobiah, who married a woman who had married seven husbands—each of whom had died on his wedding night in the bridal chamber. Not surprisingly, when she married once more, her father called in a gravedigger to prepare a new grave for his latest son-in-law.

But Tobiah was told by the angel Raphael to pray with his wife, Sarah, for deliverance before they had intercourse on their wedding night. Tobiah did exactly as he was told. "Now, Lord, you know that I take this wife of mine not because of lust, but for a noble purpose; call down your mercy on me and on her, and allow us to live together to a happy old age" (Tobit 8:7). What was the "noble purpose" of their marriage? The co-creation of new life. God answered that prayer, and Tobiah and his wife both lived to enjoy many years of married life.

In a marriage relationship we're called to obey and live God's Word. Tobiah was giving to Sarah, not just taking for his own pleasure. He asked God for His mercy, knowing that he didn't merit anything on his own. His prayer was to allow him and his wife to experience each other intimately through the sacred gift of intercourse, specifically designed for the married couple.

Men can learn a great deal by studying Tobiah's actions. Today, a man needs to ask himself what would happen if he took his wife's hand and prayed with her before intercourse. Men need to ask God to bless this time of married love, to allow the tremendous gift of co-creation to happen, if it be God's will, during the pleasurable intimacy reserved for the married couple.

Such a prayer was a powerful weapon in protecting Tobiah's marriage from death. It will do the same for the marriages of men today. Tobiah's actions demonstrate to men today that obedience to God is the core of love.

The difference between lust and love is that lust takes, while love gives. Cheryl was tired and knew Don wanted to make love, so she went beyond her feelings and encour-

*The Role of the Couple*

aged him. That was love. Don knew she was tired, but he desired her and insisted that she submit to him. That was lust.

Love is a decision to lay your life down for another. Love is a learned behavior. Love is a visible sign of the invisible presence of God who is in that person. Obedience to God is the core of love, the path to truth and the power of discipleship.

It's time for Christians to recommit themselves to the divine pattern, God's Word, our true source of authority. We're paying a terrible price for moving away from God's authority in His Word and His Church.

## Chastity

Chastity is abstinence from all unlawful sexual activity. Today we see terrible tragedies happening all over the world because of pornography, the occult and sexual perversion. Scripture calls us to obey God's commandments and abide in Him (see John 15:7). But that can't be done when chastity is being rejected.

"The unholy will not fall heir to the kingdom of God! Do not deceive yourselves: no fornicators, idolaters, or adulterers, no sodomites, thieves, misers, or drunkards, no slanderers or robbers will inherit God's kingdom" (1 Corinthians 6:9-10). Abstaining from sexual immorality is essential for entering the kingdom of heaven.

How do we remain chaste, you might ask? Through the grace of God. Thank Jesus for the cross and for dying for us to set us free. Acceptance of what Jesus did on the cross sets us free.

Scripture tells us not to associate with anyone who bears the title "brother" if he's immoral (see 1 Corinthians 5:11). It says that there must be among us no fornicators (see Hebrews 12:16). "From the mind stem evil designs—murder, adulterous conduct, fornication, stealing, false witness, blasphemy" (Matthew 15:19). Scripture tells us to not conform ourselves to this age, but to be transformed by the renewal of our mind (see Romans 12:2). We are to put on the mind of Christ (see 1 Corinthians 2:16).

When we speak about chastity, we're speaking about the virtue of purity. Chastity brings to mind whatever is pure and innocent. A chaste person is one who imitates the purity of God in all that he or she does. We're told that chastity affects our entire being, and it brings beauty and power to all God's children. To be chaste requires a strong love and deep trust in Jesus Christ, and a desire to be like Him.

The power of the Holy Spirit enables us to imitate the purity of Jesus Christ in our lives, so that we can be chaste (see Acts. 1:8). Chastity is a tremendous virtue for all God's children because it calls them to act and think in accordance with the teachings of Christ and the Church. When

## The Role of the Couple

a person talks in a manner that's lewd and sexually offensive (see Ephesians 5:3), he's offending both God and man, and he's making a mockery of his religion (see James 1:26-27). "As for lewd conduct or promiscuousness or lust of any sort, let them not even be mentioned among you; your holiness forbids this. Nor should there be any obscene, silly or suggestive talk; all that is out of place" (Ephesians 5:3-4). To be chaste is to be free of obscene talk.

When single people enter into a religious way of life, they choose to give their life to God alone with an undivided heart. This pure and unadulterated way of life, free from obscenities and sexual immorality, will continue to bring the joy of chastity to everyone around them. Their reverent way of life will be an example for others, whether married or single.

A single person who doesn't enter into a religious order is still called to be chaste. That means they must engage in no sexual intercourse outside marriage. It also means they must express chastity through the spoken word. Filthy language, swearing and dirty jokes are completely removed through the virtue of chastity. A chaste single person is a celibate person who enjoys the cleansing, healing presence of God working through his or her pure way of life.

"Let marriage be honored in every way and the marriage bed be kept undefiled, for God will judge fornicators and adulterers" (Hebrews 13:4). This scriptural text identifies what chastity is in marriage. Chastity in marriage means that both partners have to agree that whatever sexual act is performed between them is a mutually loving act that promotes unity and the possibility of creation. One partner is not being chaste when some sexual act, such as oral sex, is forced on or is repulsive to the other. Chastity requires the rejection of contraception, masturbation, abortion and pornography.

## Living With One Another

The father is the authority in the home. A man may delegate responsibility to others, but the authority is always his. Because of his authority, he'll be held accountable by God for his family life.

In a marriage relationship we're called to obey God's Word and bring its influence into every area of our lives. Scripture tells us to give ourselves humbly to God. Resist the Devil, and he will flee from you (see James 4:7). When we submit to the will of the Father, we come under the protection of the power of the Holy Spirit and the saving name of Jesus. Satan can't stand up against this kind of power and is forced to flee. We must first listen to God's Word and then obey it in order to experience the power of being one with God.

*The Role of the Couple*

Oneness grows immediately between a husband and wife when we live out the Scripture to listen to each other; to be slow to express anger; to be slow to speak; and to refrain from being defensive or abusive (see James 1:19). But we're fooling ourselves if we say we're Christians when, in reality, we can't control our sharp tongues (see James 1:26). If we don't control what we say, our actions indicate that our religion or our marriage isn't worth much to us.

On the other hand, when we stand continuously on God's Word, we're able to experience the power and protection of God Himself. After all, He has empowered us to be His children (see John 1:12). We know from our heavenly Father's point of view that when we remain true to the teaching of Jesus to love others as He loved us, then and only then does our marriage stay unsoiled by our contacts with the world (see James 1:27).

## Distortions Within the Family

Our marriage should be a reflection of the Holy Family. For that to happen, we must be crystal clear on the role of the man and the woman. The world's problem of broken marriages has become a major problem of the Church. Only God's standard makes marriage relationships and families what they need to be.

We need only to look around at our families, commu-

*Secrets of a Happy Family*

nities, cities, states and even our country to see that something is dreadfully wrong. Though most people agree that the family is the basic building block of society, still they ask, "What's wrong with the world today?" They rush to correct the problem through philosophy, education, law enforcement, more laws, even new types of religion. But the real problem we're facing is the death of marriage and the family as we know it. The family is being strangled with a chord of strands, including immorality, adultery, fornication, homosexuality, abortion, sterilization, radical feminism, juvenile delinquency and sexual rebellion.

We've heard many differing opinions about how to restructure the family and promote meaningful relationships in a disintegrating society. Yet Jesus tells us in Scripture that only the Truth can set us free (see John 8:32). Only through Him can our distortions be made into truthful reality.

## Homosexuality

Did you know that in 1973 the American Psychiatric Association removed homosexuality from its official list of psychological disorders? Yet the Scripture and the tradition of the Church clearly teach otherwise. The *Catechism of the Catholic Church* declares: "Basing itself on Sacred Scripture, which presents homosexual acts as acts of grave depravity [Romans 1:24-27], tradition has

*The Role of the Couple*

always declared that 'homosexual acts are intrinsically disordered.'. . . Under no circumstances can they be approved" (par. 2357).

Unfortunately, the homosexual cult has deeply infected our society. The people who lobby for special homosexual rights have been successful in our schools, churches and courts. We see now, to the horror of many, the ultimate insult to God our Creator: the proliferation of same-sex marriages.

Everyone needs love, and sadly, many find little or no love in this life. The pain of the person with homosexual tendencies—who turns to the counterfeit love now becoming acceptable in our society—is tragic. The struggle to find love, as Scripture describes it, is extremely difficult for the person with homosexual tendencies.

Scripture tells us that love never fails. But the search and attainment of real love can only be achieved when we learn to die to our own needs. Like all of us, the person with homosexual tendencies has a profound hunger for love. He's deprived of marriage and family life, the kind of intimacy that brings love to most human beings. This leaves the person with homosexual tendencies to embark on a lonely, frustrating and fruitless search for real love.

As the Scripture tells us, "God is love" (1 John 4:16), and only in Jesus can a true and perfect love be found. All people must turn to the place where everything and everyone is on the same level—that is, the cross. There, Jesus will give all of us the courage, strength, grace, direction and help we need to become whole. We must always remember He's our Savior; He not only forgave our sins, but also healed our diseases (see Psalm 103:3). He told us clearly that He came to seek out those who are lost (see Luke 19:10).

## Submission to One Another

The *Catechism* reminds us: "Having become a member of the Church, the person baptized belongs no longer to himself, but to Him who died and rose for us" (par. 1269). In belonging to Him, we must "defer to one another out of reverence for Christ" (Ephesians 5:21).

When we love another person, we are in effect loving Christ. A loving embrace, a gentle kiss, a warm hello are all offered not only to a family member or friend, but also to Christ. As God's children, we must acknowledge that we're heirs of His Kingdom. Through our baptism, we've entered into that kingdom.

God the Father, the Son and the Holy Spirit now resides in each one of us. We have in fact become temples of the Holy Spirit. If God is present in all His children, then to be involved with other people is to be involved with God Himself.

## The Role of the Couple

When we ignore our spouse, a child of God, aren't we also ignoring the God who lives in that spouse as His temple? When we neglect our parents, we dishonor not only them, but also God. If we provoke our children, we insult not only our children, but also God. To be a real servant leader, we must always defer to others as if deferring to God Himself.

We see in Scripture how Christ deferred to us in the same manner as He deferred to His Father: Jesus took on the role of a slave, allowing himself to be ridiculed, assaulted and even put to death on a cross because His Father's plan called Him to this level of love. We can only be genuine when we're deferring to others as if we were deferring to Christ Himself.

When, for example, a single man looks at a woman with respect rather than lust, he defers to Christ as well as to the woman. When a married man dies to his needs and attends to his wife's needs first, he defers to Christ.

Christ proved His love by dying for us while we were still sinning, and we're called to do the same. This means accepting others despite their faults and sinfulness. Does that seem difficult? Just keep in mind that God has a tremendous sense of humor. If you don't believe it, just look in the mirror.

Here's an example of this principle of deferring to another person as to Christ. Marie went ballistic recently over

*Secrets of a Happy Family*

an episode in our daily routine. We had been traveling all day and we were both tired. She had offered to drive because the pain in Ken's spine and back was miserable. When we got in the car, Ken pulled out a newspaper and began to read while she was driving.

As Ken was reading, he heard a low growl from the depths of some unknown abyss say, "I am *not* your chauffeur appointed to drive while you read." That description may sound humorous, but when Ken looked up at Marie, what he saw in her eyes was definitely not funny.

In effect, Marie was saying, "Don't shut me out and treat me as if I'm some stranger serving as your chauffeur." She wanted her husband to communicate with her.

The bottom line was this: If Christ had been riding in that van with Ken, would he have taken up the newspaper to read and left Him sitting there lonely? If not, why would Ken do that to Marie? We're called to defer to one another as if to Christ.

Many times the spouse, parent or caregiver of a chronically ill person suffers from a one-sided relationship. In other words, one gives most of the time and the other takes most of the time. This has often been the case for us because of Ken's illness: Marie for many years has tried to make his constant pain and discomfort as acceptable as can be. She gives even when she's tired or, in many cases, not feeling good herself. Nevertheless, she has needs too, and they should be met first, as far as possible, by her husband.

The role of the married man and woman is akin to the role of Christ and His Church. A husband is to love his wife as Christ loves his bride, the Church. He is to suffer and even die for her as Christ died for his bride. She is to affirm, support, and encourage him.

A man leaves the comfort and love given him by his parents so he can cling to his wife. Now he's to give her comfort and love; he's to give and stop taking. Men who don't give up taking from their parents don't know how to give to their wives. Often their marriages are destroyed.

## Covenant vs. contract

A marriage is a *covenant* between God and a husband and wife, who form a living trinity, a holy three. That's different from a mere contract. A covenant governs relationships, while a contract only administers things.

In a contract, man is the guarantor. A contract guaranteed by man is subject to revocation when the guarantor doesn't get what's promised. For example, when you buy a car, you may sign a contract to make thirty-six payments. If you miss a few payments, the car is taken back. The contract is then broken.

In a covenant, however, God is the Guarantor, and He never breaks His Word. He loves you forever, and His covenant is forever. We find an example of such a covenant with God in Jeremiah 31:3: "With age-old love I have loved you, so I have kept my mercy toward you." It doesn't matter what you do; He still loves you.

Without being yoked with Christ, man can make only a contract, and it often ends in divorce. In a divorce God doesn't break His part of the covenant; man does. That's why even a divorced person can continue his personal covenant with God.

## Role Model

St. Joseph showed tremendous obedience to God when faced with the apparent violation of his betrothal to Mary. Joseph must have been devastated at the news of Mary's pregnancy. He was a righteous man and a devout observer of the law of Moses. He didn't want to shame or punish her. He merely wanted to divorce her quietly and get on with his life.

Nevertheless, the angel of the Lord appeared to him in a dream and told him that Mary hadn't betrayed him. Mary had conceived a Child through the Holy Spirit. His wife would bear a Son, and his name would be called Jesus.

Joseph believed the angel and chose to take her as his wife. This act of *obedience* was made in the face of the embarrassment both Joseph and Mary would experience in their community. When Joseph took her into his home, "he had no relations with her at any time before she bore a

*The Role of the Couple*

son, whom he named Jesus" (Matthew 1:25).

Just think about this situation: Joseph was a young man who married a warm, loving, beautiful young woman. Jewish law allowed him to have sex with his wife. It wasn't only legal; it was natural. Yet he died to his sexual needs and didn't enter into a sexual union with Mary. He *obeyed* God even when such obedience made demands beyond his normal role as a husband.

What tremendous faith, humility and strength in God this man had! Both he and Mary were chaste; and in our day as in their day, chastity is still the center of a holy family. Men can look to St. Joseph for help in their own marriages. A strong, loving marriage is one of the closest things to a piece of heaven on earth.

## Questions for Reflection

- How can we love one another just as Christ loved the Church?
- How have I exercised my gift of chastity with regard to my spouse or the Church?
- How can I submit to my spouse out of reverence to Christ?

## Application of the Lesson

*Ephesians 5:21:* "Defer to one another out of reverence for Christ."

Practice deferring to one another. Find specific ways to defer, and each day, identify and write down one way you have deferred to your spouse.

Let us pray:

Lord, thank You for showing us how to be one in You. Help us to defer to one another out of reverence for You. We commit our lives and our relationship into Your loving hands to do with as You will. Amen.

## CHAPTER FIVE
# THE ROLE OF THE PARENTS
## Parenting Responsibilities

The primary responsibility of a father and mother is to be teachers and to transmit the love they have for one another to their children and others. They are to teach the child a sense of obedience, discipline, reverence and respect for all lawful authority.

A single parent has the most demanding role in the Christian kingdom. He or she is called to be both mother and father to the children and to be true to him or herself as well. A single parent experiences many responsibilities and much loneliness. Where possible, other members of the extended family should help out, become additional mentors and role models for the children.

Pope John Paul II gives single parents much encouragement when he states: "Loneliness and other difficulties are often the lot of separated spouses, especially when they are the innocent parties. The ecclesial community must support such people more than ever. It must give them much respect, solidarity, understanding and practical help, so that they can preserve their fidelity even in their diffi-

*Secrets of a Happy Family*

cult situation; and it must help them to cultivate the need to forgive, which is inherent in Christian love, and to be ready perhaps to return to their former married life."[12]

The role of parenthood continues when parents become grandparents. Grandparents many times are moral and spiritual leaders in their families and communities. They have achieved this level of respect through their years of responsibility, trust and experience.

A grandparent tends to look at a child almost as God does in that nothing shocks God and everything is within His scope of mercy and forgiveness. Pope John Paul II says about the elderly in the family: "There are cultures which manifest a unique veneration and great love for the elderly: Far from being outcasts from the family or merely tolerated as a useless burden, they continue to be present and to take an active and responsible part in family life; though having to respect the autonomy of the new family, above all they carry out the important mission of being a witness to the past and a source of wisdom for the young and for the future."[13]

We're told in Scripture that for the child to honor his father and mother (see Exodus 20:12) is the key to the parent-child relationship. When a child grows up in an atmosphere of love, discipline, honor and respect for both parents and grandparents, then that child is prepared for success in many kinds of human relationships. "How many

## The Role of the Parents

children," the Holy Father observes, "have found understanding and love in the eyes and words and caresses of the aging! And how many old people have willingly subscribed to the inspired word that the 'crown of the aged is their children's children.' Proverbs 17:6 states: 'Grandchildren are the crown of old men, and the glory of children is their parentage.'"[14]

To understand the seriousness of this matter, we should consider certain provisions of the Old Testament law. It required that "whoever strikes his father or mother shall be put to death" (Exodus 21:15), and if a child even cursed his mother or father, that child had to be put to death (see Exodus 21:17). Why is this matter so critical? Because a person's relations to others as a whole and for a lifetime are largely based on what he was taught as a child in the home. If a child learns love, honor, discipline and respect from his parents, he'll be blessed throughout his life.

The result of faulty teaching by parents is often an undisciplined child without respect for authority or honor toward his parents and grandparents. Such a lack of proper child rearing can increase disorder in an already disorderly world.

As parents we are to treat our children in the same way our heavenly Father treats us. He provides, protects, educates, trains, corrects and disciplines us. All that our heavenly Father does for us is based on His great love

*Secrets of a Happy Family*

for us. All that we do for our children should be based on the great love we have for them as well.

Just as our heavenly Father guides us as His children, we parents must guide our own children. But we have to be aware of our heavenly Father's plan of action before we can imitate it in raising our own children.

Today there's widespread rebellion of children against their parents. Countless books and therapy programs try to deal with this issue. Such a breakdown between parent and child is a serious indictment of our society. The family is disintegrating right before our very eyes.

We're told in Scripture that people perish for lack of knowledge (see Hosea 4:6). This charge was made by the prophets against the leaders of God's community—not the followers. Since we're the leaders of our families, the charge applies to us as well. We must have the proper knowledge of how to raise children. But if we haven't been properly taught, how can we teach our children?

The failure to pass on to our children what our heavenly Father has taught us lies primarily with the father. His responsibility is to become a man of God's Word and lead his wife into the Word. Then they both share the responsibility of bringing their children into a personal relationship with Christ through the Word.

*The Role of the Parents*

Where do we start? The following are some guidelines from our heavenly Father that we in turn need to pass on to our children.

## Teaching

How can we burn God's Word into our hearts and the hearts of our children? The Scripture tells us: We must carefully teach the commandments of God to our children and talk about them often—when we're at home, and when we go out; at bedtime, and the first thing in the morning. Tie the commandments on your fingers, the Bible says; wear them on your forehead, and write them on the door posts of your home (see Deuteronomy 6:4-9).

God encourages us to teach His Word at *any and every time.* When a child grows up knowing, because of such teaching, that both his heavenly Father and his earthly father love him, such a child will likely become a person of honor and reverence for God, family and country.

## Protection

From what does God protect us? God protects us from evil: "The Lord keeps faith; He it is who will strengthen you and guard you against the evil one" (2 Thessalonians 3:3).

When Jesus' disciples asked Him how to pray, He taught them the Our Father (see Matthew 6:13). In that prayer, as children of God we come to Him asking Him to "deliver us from the evil one." He is always there and answers our prayer.

So many times we're tempted in everyday situations. The Devil invites us to overeat, or tell a little white lie on our income tax, or let the sun set on our anger. We forget to turn to God and ask for His protection from such temptation, so we end up falling into Satan's trap.

Nevertheless, all it takes is asking Him to deliver us from the temptation, and He'll do it for us. He tells us: "Ask, and you will receive; seek, and you will find; knock, and it shall be opened to you" (see Matthew 7:7). God will always give us a way out when we're tempted. He won't let us be tested beyond our strength (see 1 Corinthians 10:13).

Many times Satan tempts us through the entertainment media, such as TV, movies and the Internet. We recall how recently we went to see a movie that was rated P.G. One of the characters in it used the Lord's name in vain. We hesitated about leaving, hoping the merits of a good plot would outweigh the offensive language. But when the name Jesus Christ was used again, without any indication that He is our Lord and Savior, we walked out. The Lord always gives us a way out; we only need to pray and then do what He calls us to do.

As parents, we protect our children by not allowing

*The Role of the Parents*

them to watch movies or TV programs with content that contradicts the teachings of Jesus Christ. This is in fact probably the greatest way to protect them today. We also protect them by being very aware of what's being taught in their schools, especially in sex education programs. If the curriculum doesn't conform to God's Word, we must have the courage to protect our children by putting them in schools where conformance to God's Word is taught. Another excellent alternative is home schooling.

God also protects us against persecution. He will keep us safe in the time of trial that's coming on the whole world (see Revelation 3:10). He gives us the words to speak when we're being persecuted (see Matthew 10:17-20).

The Lord protects us against our enemies. Who are our enemies? We're not fighting against flesh and blood but against rulers, against authorities, against the powers of the dark world and against the spiritual forces of evil in the heavenly realms (see Ephesians 6:12). Satan has entered into the hearts of our rulers and authorities, with the result that they push for the acceptance of contraception, abortion and homosexuality.

As parents, we need to stand firm in the Truth, Jesus. Jesus says, "I am the Way, the Truth, and the Life" (John 14:6). We need to be in a right place with God. As His children we need to listen and obey Him. We're to be at peace and ready to give that peace to others wherever it

*Secrets of a Happy Family*
will be received.

We must be faithful in all we say and do. We're saved by the blood of Jesus; we're to proclaim and live out every word that comes forth from the mouth of God. He protects us from danger (see Psalm 91:3-7). He takes away our fear of what is to come and of what is taking place right now. "Perfect love casts out fear, because fear has to do with punishment" (1 John 4:18). When you come to know that God loves you and that He lives within you—when you come to recognize His presence in you—fear goes away.

## Training

Our heavenly Father trains us in varying ways, but whatever the type of training we receive, it's all for one purpose: to make us into children who show Him how much we love Him by the way we love others. God tells us in Scripture to love Him with all our heart, soul and strength. He tells us to take these words into our heart. In other words, we can't let them go in one ear and out the other (see Deuteronomy 6:4-5).

The Lord also tells us to *drill* His words into our minds so that we become deeply familiar with them. Military training includes drills, both to increase the troops' understanding of their function and to increase their skills. In a similar way, God tells parents to speak His words repeatedly,

## The Role of the Parents

whether we're at home or away, whether we're busy or at rest. A team that trains together constantly is a team that will succeed.

God's Word tells us that, for such spiritual and moral training, all Scripture is good and inspired by God (see 2 Timothy 3:16). Our heavenly Father wants His children to become holy as He is holy. In the same way, we must want our children to become holy and to hunger for God's holy Word.

Carol was raised by parents who were evenly yoked in Christ (see 2 Corinthians 6:14). To be evenly yoked means to follow the teachings of Jesus Christ *together*. Carol was trained to pray with the family at meal times. She went to church every Sunday with her parents and to Christian classes during the week. She became more active in her spiritual training as she got older.

Carol became a Christian counselor at the seminar program known as Christian Youth Encounters. She shared with her community a gifted voice as she sang spiritual songs. Although she went through various stages of teenage rebellion, that rebellion was always counter-balanced by the training she'd received from her parents.

Sadly, Carol was struck down in her last year of high school by a life-threatening disease. All the training she received from her parents and church were severely put to the test. She reached into her deposit of faith and discov-

*Secrets of a Happy Family*

ered that Jesus was the Source of supply for all her needs (see Philippians 4:19). She also found that she could endure anything with Christ (see Philippians 4:13).

Carol recovered from her illness and married a man who also had received spiritual training from his parents. Carol and Joe have been evenly yoked in that *together* they follow the teachings of Jesus. They now are training their five children in His teachings in the same spirit that their heavenly Father taught their earthly parents.

## Discipline

How does God our Father correct us? "All Scripture is inspired by God, and is useful for teaching, for refutation, for correction, and for training in righteousness" (2 Timothy 3:16). We see here that God corrects us through Scripture.

Conversion can take place, for example, when we read the biblical chapter on love (1 Corinthians 13). The Lord corrects us by showing us that keeping a record of all the ways we've been wronged by others and brooding over our injuries is detrimental not only to us, but also to those who have wronged us. Scripture corrects our "stinkin' thinkin'" by telling us not to conform to the present age, but to renew our minds (see Romans 12:2).

Wrong thinking has been passed on to us through our friends, parents and the media. So we must renew our minds

*The Role of the Parents*

by filling them with thoughts that are good, clean and pure (see Philippians 4:8). This brings us a calmness and peace that surpasses all understanding (see Philippians 4:7).

## Correction

Correction is also part of our heavenly Father's plan for us. He tells us in Scripture, "For whom the Lord loves He reproves, and He chastises the son He favors" (Proverbs 3:12). God tells us in this verse that as a Father, He corrects His son because He loves him. Today many children are being denied the protection of a father's love because their earthly fathers don't take time to correct them. The only correction many of them ever receive comes after they're adults—in a state prison. An example follows.

Jack came from a home where there was very little spiritual and moral training. He was told to go to church, but his parents never went there with him. He received some training from the church, but it was contradicted by what he saw in the lives of the people there. The training from his family was without love or example.

When Jack did something wrong, his father often wasn't around. His mother made up excuses for Jack. At first, she thought he was being cute. Meanwhile, Jack became a little smarter and didn't get caught anymore.

Discipline was rarely applied. Whenever Jack said or did something wrong, someone bailed him out, usually his

*Secrets of a Happy Family*

mother. As he got older, they said he was just "high-spirited." From his perspective, his problems in high school and college stemmed from the teachers' failure to understand him — and his mother agreed with him.

Today, Jack is in a California state prison doing time because the state refused to accept his crime of rape as "cute" behavior. Jack never had an earthly father who learned from his heavenly Father how to give his son godly correction.

If God corrects us through Scripture, how very important it is that we as parents know Scripture well enough to correct our children using it.

John's teenage son came home from a party late one night, trying to sneak in without waking his father and mother. He was so drunk he was making all kinds of noise. John was aware of his son's actions, but he didn't say anything that night.

The next day, however, John showed his son from Scripture that the drunkard and the glutton come to poverty (see Proverbs 23:21). He told him that an addiction to alcohol or drugs could rob him of all his money. One day even it could make him lose, not just all his material possessions, but his soul as well.

John showed him this scriptural passage: "Do you not know that the unjust will not inherit the kingdom of God? Do not be deceived: neither fornicators nor idolaters nor adulterers, nor boy prostitutes nor sodomites nor thieves

*The Role of the Parents*

nor the greedy nor drunkards nor slanderers nor robbers will inherit the kingdom of God" (1 Corinthians 6:9-10).

John did several things in this situation that deserve consideration. First, he waited until the next morning to talk to his son because he knew that he couldn't reason with a drunkard. He also wanted to speak to his son without being angry, and he needed the time to cool off. John waited to speak to his son so he would speak with scriptural authority and a father's love.

Second, John told his son that what he did was unacceptable, not just in his home but also in God's kingdom. His father's expressed concern was not only for his son's physical safety but, more importantly, for his spiritual safety.

Third, when John finished correcting his son, he made sure the young man understood that no matter what happened, his father would always love him. John was following the example of God Himself: Only when we know how much our heavenly Father loves us are we capable of becoming truly loving parents.

## Provision

When parents are asked what provision their children need most, the answer often is "a college education." They're willing to make great sacrifices to put their children through college. And why do they want their children to go to college? Many parents believe it's necessary to get a good job and make good money. They think that this is what it means to provide for their children.

Other parents may think they're to provide their child with the opportunity to become a famous athlete. Asked why, the answer is the same: So he can make lots of money.

But those aren't God's priorities. Our heavenly Father wants to provide for His children something far beyond education, fame and money. He wants His children to live forever, believing in His only-begotten Son and sharing in His eternal life (see John 3:16).

How does God our Father provide for us? He provides for us, as we find in Genesis, by giving us the trees and other seed-bearing plants, the rain and the sun to help the plants grow, and all the natural provisions of this world. Before Adam and Eve sinned, food and shelter were easily obtained. All Adam had to do was cultivate and care for what God had provided.

God still provides us with all we need; yet because of sin, pollution and destruction of some of the good things God has provided, all we need isn't so easily obtained. We have to work "by the sweat of our brow" to keep shoes on the feet of our children, food on the table, and a roof over our head.

Nevertheless, if we cultivate and care for what God has given us, we'll experience God's provision and receive the shelter, clothes and food our children need (see Gen-

## The Role of the Parents

esis chapter 1). Since God is love, He also is able to provide all the love we need. As we noted before, we as parents should provide our children with the same love God provides for us. God provides us a way out from all our trials so that we may be able to bear it (see 1 Corinthians 10:13).

Alice is a loving, generous and forgiving person. God provided her, through adoption, a loving family who accepted her with complete openness and love. Alice wasn't a loner as a child, but in high school she began getting into trouble, and her grades dropped. Although she still went to church on Sundays, some unwisely-chosen friends came to dominate her life. When at home, she stayed in her room and wouldn't allow anyone to bother her.

God provided Alice, through her parents, the opportunity to go college. She dropped out in her first year. She had a difficult time being trustworthy, and the trust so necessary for family life was shattered. The lives of her parents slowly turned into a nightmare.

Once grown into a young woman, Alice allowed men in her life who used her, abused her and then threw her away. She left home and went through some heart-breaking times. After falling into a few destructive relation-

*Secrets of a Happy Family*

ships, she dropped completely out of sight.

During these years her parents prayed for her every day. When she finally contacted them again, they told her they had always loved her and would continue to love her, but they hated what she was doing to herself and to others. Her parents were concerned for her safety and for her soul.

Alice's lifestyle, the kind that's accepted by the world, leads to despair, destruction and even death because "the wages of sin is death" (Romans 6:23). Her father showed her from Scripture that, among others, fornicators will not enter the kingdom of heaven (see 1 Corinthians 6:9-11). He explained that fornicators are those who engage in sexual intercourse outside of marriage.

Alice eventually married a man who abused her emotionally, physically and sexually. One day she even needed hospital care because of a severe beating he gave her. Alice called her parents from the emergency room. They were relieved and grateful to God, not just that she was alive, but that they had another chance to communicate with her.

Alice ended up divorced, yet continued to get involved with other men. Meanwhile, God had provided her with parents who were there whenever she called for help. They helped her by giving the love and support she needed at the time. Because of them, Alice also had a background

## The Role of the Parents

of good training and education in the Lord that could help her in her journey to the truth.

Today, God and Alice's family continue to provide her with love and support. She's now engaged to be married. If she marries a man with whom she's evenly yoked, she'll likely experience the love and peace that only God can give to all those who obey him. Scripture tells us that God provides a way out of our troubles (see 1 Corinthians 10:13). Alice's parents pray that she will take God up on that promise and return to the kingdom, not just part of the way, but completely.

We're told not to rely on our wealth, but on God. He richly provides us with all things for our enjoyment (see 1 Timothy 6:17). Bob learned the lesson about relying on wealth the hard way. His marriage ended in divorce because he married a woman with whom he wasn't evenly yoked.

They both were making good money. In the first year of marriage, they bought a new home and two cars, and Bob's wife became pregnant. They had twins. When an economic recession hit, Bob was laid off his job. Panic, depression and a loss of material possessions resulted.

Bob's wife divorced him as he struggled to find work. As depressed and devastated as he was after the divorce, he never wavered from his faith in God. He continued to go to church and seek emotional support from his family.

*Secrets of a Happy Family*

Whenever he had custody of his children, he took them to church, providing them with the faith and love that had been passed on to him.

Bob is learning now that he can't put his trust in money, because money may be temporary. He's put his hope in the Lord and received the love God provided for him through Jesus. As he continues to seek help from the Lord, the Lord continues to give him direction. Faith, hope, and love abide in Bob's life, and the greatest of these is the love that God has provided (see 1 Corinthians 13:13).

## Endowments of Our Father

How does our heavenly Father *educate* us here on Earth? We learn through the *teachings* of Jesus Christ and the Church and through the power of the Holy Spirit. St. Paul sends out a reminder that rings true even today: "Brothers, stand firm. Hold fast to the traditions you received from us, either by our word or by letter" (2 Thessalonians 2:15).

Scripture also warns us against being misled by false teachers, some of whom even come speaking in Jesus' name (see Luke 21:8). God promised us through the prophet Isaiah: "All your sons shall be taught by the Lord, and great shall be the peace of your children" (Isaiah 54:13). What a comfort and blessing this is to His sons who are alive today!

We read in the Scripture that God loves those He *re-*

## The Role of the Parents

*proves*. He delights in us. But we may get upset when He chastises, because our education, status and wealth have made us too proud to be open to humbling experiences.

God is a loving Father who is always ready to *protect* His children against any type of danger. Scripture tells us that He will strengthen us in our battle against Satan. We're no match against Satan when we're alone, but with the aid of our loving Father, we become victorious (see 2 Thessalonians 3:3).

"No test has been sent to you that does not come to all men" (1 Corinthians 10:13). We may think no one else has ever gone through such an ordeal as we've experienced. But sooner or later we find that many have been where we are right now, and they not only made it through their time of trial—they became better for it.

This is the strength and protection our heavenly Father promises us. He is a God who delivers on all His promises. He will always show us a way out of every situation. He is our loving Father who wants us to call out to Him in time of danger.

Our heavenly Father *protects* us from stumbling when we're weak and begin to fall. He helps us to stand unblemished and exult in the presence of His glory. He makes us revel in the fact that He chose us to be His children. His love for us is so great that He'll do anything to prevent us from destruction. All we have to do is call out to Him; He'll never turn us away (see John 6:37).

Our beloved Father *trains* us in this short earthly life through Scripture (see 2 Timothy 3:16). All Scripture is useful for teaching us how to live in His kingdom. He shows us how to accept constructive criticism and teaches us humility and obedience in our daily training. He also shows us how to become holy through obedience to the command of all those who are in lawful authority, such as parents, teachers, clergy and government officials, unless what they require of us would be contrary to Jesus' teachings.

Sometimes when discipline is applied to us, it seems to bring more grief than joy. But in due time it will bring forth the fruit of peace and justice to those who are raised up in this type of training (see Hebrews 12:11). We can see from Scripture how our Father trains us up in many different areas. His protection, training, education, correction and provision are unmistakable signs of a loving Father.

## The Father: Fulfillment of All Our Needs

Here, then, is a blueprint for earthly parents to love their children as our heavenly Father loves us. When we read in Psalm 18:2 that the Lord is our Rock, our Fortress, and our Deliverer, it should give us great courage and hope.

*The Role of the Parents*

We can visualize a strong loving Father standing watch over His young child.

We see God as our loving Father, Someone we can run to, in whose arms we can hide ourselves completely. We can take refuge in His strength, courage and gentleness. We know that His love is our shield against the fiery darts of evil and pain in our world.

Nowhere else do we experience the peace we have when we're with our heavenly Father in prayer. He is our Stronghold and our Salvation. He's the Father we may have never experienced as a child or even as an adult. He's always just what we need at any moment.

When we're children, He's tall, strong and happy. When we become adults, He's always waiting for us to stop and say hello to Him. When we call on Him, He always has time for us and He never interrupts us. He listens, He smiles and He cries. We notice His hands are always extended toward us.

Even now in our adulthood we still want to run into His arms and have those loving hands hold us close to Him. We can still see clearly His hands resting on our heads as He blesses us. He will always be our Father, He will always be our Rock, our Fortress and our Deliverer. We will always be His children, His delightful children, and His love will endure forever.

*Secrets of a Happy Family*

## Questions for Reflection

- In what areas do I need to strengthen my role as a parent?
- How am I a role model as a parent?
- How has God provided for, protected and disciplined me?

## Application of the Lesson

*Proverbs 22:6:* "Train a boy in the way he should go; even when he is old, he will not swerve from it."

*Philippians 4:8:* "Your thoughts should be wholly directed to all that is true, all that deserves respect, all that is honest, pure, admirable, decent, virtuous or worthy of praise."

Correct and train your children by applying a specific scriptural text to each situation, such as the passage above from Philippians: "You can't watch that TV program or go to that movie because it will fill your mind with bad things, and God is telling us to fill our minds with what is good."

Let us pray:

Lord, thank You for taking care of me and always providing me a way out of my troubles. Help me to be a role model to my children by imitating You. Help me always to guide them to You in thought, word and deed. Amen

## CHAPTER SIX
# THE ROLE OF THE CHILDREN
## Children of Our Heavenly Father

We approached the role of the parent from the perspective of how God treats us as our Father. Now we'll consider the role of children: first, viewing the parents as adult children of our heavenly Father; and second, viewing children's responsibility to their earthly father. Children are to respond to the authority given by God to their earthly parents with obedience, respect, reverence and honor. A child honors his parents by *listening to them and obeying them.* As an adult we must respond in the same way to our heavenly Father.

### Baptism and rebirth in Christ

Who are the children of God? "Any who did accept Him He empowered to become children of God" (John 1:12). Jesus said, "I assure you, unless you change and become like little children, you will not enter the kingdom of God" (Matthew 18:3). "Let the children come to me. Do not hinder them. The kingdom of God belongs to such as these" (Matthew 19:14).

*Secrets of a Happy Family*

How do we identify the children of God? To become children of God, we must be baptized and reborn in Christ. Jesus told Nicodemus, "No one can enter into God's kingdom without being begotten from above" (John 3:5). The *Catechism* explains: "Through baptism we are freed from sin and reborn as sons of God; we become members of Christ, are incorporated into the Church and made sharers in her mission: 'Baptism is the sacrament of regeneration through water in the word'" (par. 1213).

Many of us were brought into the family of God as babies through baptism. Later we made that personal acceptance and submission to Christ in our lives by following the lead of His Spirit. Through our obedience to Church authorities we, as children of God, are led by His Spirit to Jesus.

Jesus has given us His presence here on earth through His Spirit dwelling in those who have accepted His call. As we defer to one another out of reverence for Christ, we are in reality deferring to God Himself out of reverence for His Son. When we submit to those in authority and obey them, we are, in turn, submitting to and obeying God. When we listen, submit and obey, we're honoring our heavenly Father and following the lead of His Spirit.

When we're baptized into Christ and experience His Holy Spirit's presence in us, we begin our life and walk as children of God.

## Training and discipline

God disciplined Adam when He expelled him from the garden: "The Lord God therefore banished him from the garden of Eden, to till the ground from which he had been taken" (Genesis 3:23). We too will be disciplined by the Lord when we're disobedient and refuse to confess our sin, just as Adam failed to confess his sin.

When Marie looks back to her infancy of walking with the Lord, she can see how she needed to be fed spiritual "baby food" as she learned how to digest God's Word so she could obey her heavenly Father. She recalls much kicking, screaming and rebelling in those days. Wanting to do things her way, she had to be corrected often because of her rebellion. It took years of training by the Church and submission to it before she learned the meaning of true honor, of trusting in God as He works through His people, the Church.

As a child trusts in his parents to provide for him, we trust in our heavenly Father working through the Church to provide for us. We trust our heavenly Father through the Church to protect us. We believe our heavenly Father when He tells us He will protect us, and He will never leave us nor forsake us.

We believe God when He tells us He will do what He says in His Word. "So is my word, that goes out from my mouth; it will not return to me empty, but will accomplish what I desire" (Isaiah 55:11). He disciplines us through the Church.

Marie has been trained and educated through God's Word. As she grows in her journey she discovers that His Spirit, working through the Church, has led her to the truth. Being under the protection of the Church, she hasn't gone astray, doing her own thing instead of God's thing.

She's mindful of the warning: "For lack of guidance a people falls; security lies in many counselors" (Proverbs 11:14). Through the Church God has corrected her and led her on the path of holiness. "Our earthly fathers disciplined us for a little while as they thought best; but God disciplines us for our good, that we may share in his holiness" (Hebrews 12:10). To accept our spiritual leaders who hand down the teachings of Jesus Christ, as the Apostles did, is to accept Christ. To reject our spiritual leaders is to reject Christ Himself.

It's essential for us, as children of God, to spend time alone with God to hear His voice. This is the time to get up in His lap and let Him hold us. We're all sheep who have gone astray. He's looking for His lost sheep, and when He finds them, He picks them up and carries them home.

## Obedience

We show reverence and honor by obeying God. Yet

## The Role of the Children

obedience is probably one of the most difficult tasks for us because the human will is so stubborn.

As children of God, we are to obey all lawful authority. We are to show reverence and honor to our parents even when they get old. Children are always to respect and submit to lawful authority. "Let everyone obey the authorities that are over him, for there is no authority except from God, and all authority that exists is established by God" (Romans 13:1).

Of course, if lawful authority is in disobedience to our heavenly Father's authority, we are always to obey God and not man (see Acts 5:29). If we are to put our full trust in God working through the Church, that is, His Holy Spirit working through man, then it's essential that we as children of God learn His ways. We must come to know Jesus, our Brother, in the Word.

When as children we shared a house with earthly brothers and sisters, we came to know them rather well. Living under the same roof, we knew more or less the way they would act and respond in certain situations. In a similar way, as we live under the roof of our heavenly Father and come to know Jesus, our Brother, intimately—abiding in him—then we're able to distinguish God's way from man's way. That discernment then enables us to follow and obey God rather than man.

To sum up, we show honor and reverence for our heavenly Father when we listen and obey His Son working through men by His Holy Spirit.

## Children's Responsibility to Their Earthly Father
## Listening and obeying

God's children show their love for Him through obedience to His Word and to all lawful authority. In the same way, children are to listen and obey parents and Church authority. The role of children is to ask questions and learn the ways of God, just as Jesus did as a twelve-year-old boy in the temple (see Luke 2:47).

## Example setting by parents

We're told in Scripture that it's better to obey God than man (see Acts 5:29). Today this principle is difficult even for an adult, let alone a child. Most children follow what could be called a "monkey see, monkey do" theology.

Children may or may not understand much of what we say, but they generally will imitate much of what we do. If they see us obeying the rules of God, they will likely obey His rules as well. If they see us obey the rules of man, they will likely obey those rules too. Let's look at a few examples.

Johnny is being mean to his sister, so his dad slaps him

## The Role of the Children

for his behavior. On another occasion Johnny observes little sister being mean. What do you think Johnny will do? He probably will imitate his dad's violent act. If, on the other hand, his dad had taken him aside and corrected him privately, explaining that he was being disciplined because of his inappropriate behavior toward his sister, Johnny would have been more likely to understand the call to obedience and gained better insight into dealing with someone who's creating a problem.

The best way children learn obedience to God is by observing their parents and older brothers and sisters practice it.

Sally is with her mother in the shopping center helping her put the bags in the auto. Sally notices an article she doesn't recall having paid for. She shows the item to her mother, who checks her sales slip and finds that Sally is correct.

Mom then tells her daughter that it's not theirs. Because God tells us in the sixth commandment, "Thou shall not steal," they must return it. She shows her daughter by her action that she's being obedient to God, not man. What impression do you think this leaves on her daughter?

Children raised by parents who provide clear examples of obedience to God can become persons who are really free. They're able to make decisions based on their own experiences of obedience to God.

Jesus is a role model for children. Scripture states

*Secrets of a Happy Family*

little about Jesus as a Child. However, as a twelve-year-old, He set an example of listening and asking questions (see Luke 2:46). "Jesus grew up in strength and wisdom" (Luke 2:40). He also was obedient to His parents (see John 2:51).

As a Boy in the temple with learned men, Jesus asked deep questions, and they were impressed with His knowledge and understanding. A young man of His age was expected to be obedient and learn the sacred Word. They presumed that He must have spent a great deal of time studying Scripture, because His obedience and knowledge suggested that He studied faithfully.

Children who grow up in an atmosphere of obedience learn the truth at an early age. Therefore, they become capable of loving others, because the core of all love is obedience. Love is giving; love is service; an obedient person is one who willingly gives.

Children must depend on those in charge for their chance to become what God has called us to be, and that is to be saved. Truth is reality, not as *we* perceive it, but as it really is. Truth is Jesus Christ, yesterday, today, and tomorrow (see Hebrews 13:8).

Children who habitually hear lies or half-truths may well become liars. Children who hear only the truth have the foundation to become truthful, obedient persons. Children who are taught to live and act as Jesus did will

*The Role of the Children*

likely be obedient, loving children.

Today, many children from good homes, trained in the way of the Lord, are swayed by peer pressure to deviate into alcohol, drugs and promiscuity. Eventually, perhaps after years of prayer by their parents, many come back to what they were taught as children. Often they come back and resume their growth in the Lord, sometimes right where they left off.

Cathy was a bright, cheerful, lovely young Christian girl who deviated from her walk with Christ, going down a path of destruction. She knew God's Word; she went to Christian schools; she was from a family that loved her; and yet she fell away from much she had learned. She shattered the trust and friendship she had enjoyed with her entire family.

Lies led to disobedience, which in turn led to rebellion. In a very short time this young teenager was well into alcohol and drugs. Her marks in school dropped dramatically as she listened to her peers instead of her parents. On one occasion she even stole the family auto to meet with friends after her family had gone to bed.

Cathy's continued path of rebellion caused her to be thrown out of college. She became involved in several traumatic relationships with various men. Eventually, she entered a marriage filled with physical abuse that ended in divorce.

At last, however, Cathy has turned away from Satan

*Secrets of a Happy Family*

and turned back to God. She's picking up the pieces of her life and, through her faith in God and her family's prayer, she appears to stand a good chance of once again becoming a whole person.

Another example of what can happen is Paul, a little boy diagnosed with learning and coordination problems who came from a family with a strong faith in God. He was deeply loved by his parents and siblings. But his dad was intense in his expectations, and in trying to help his son overcome his problems, he in fact made them worse.

Paul tried hard, but it seemed as if he could never jump high enough, kick far enough, or run fast enough for his dad. So the boy grew up angry and frustrated. When he was old enough to be on his own, his lack of self-esteem led him into alcohol, drunk driving and a traumatic divorce.

Through prayer and faith, Paul's father eventually recognized the intense pressure he'd put on his son and the damage it had done. It took time, but both men began to change. Today the son is growing closer and closer to his father through the faith and prayers of the whole family.

Growing up learning God's Word can greatly increase children's faith and obedience—and children like that can change our world as we know it today. Scripture tells us to go out and make disciples of all nations (see Matthew 23:19). This takes a great deal of obedience on the part of

*The Role of the Children*

both parents and children, but the reward is great: peace of heart and mind in this world, and eternal life in the next.

## Becoming persons of honor

Scripture tells us, "Honor your father and your mother" (Exodus 20:12). In the *Catechism* we read: "The divine fatherhood is the source of human fatherhood; this is the foundation of the honor owed to parents. The respect of children, whether minors or adults, for their father and mother is nourished by the natural affection born of the bond uniting them. It is required by God's commandment" (par. 2214).

The word "honor" implies that what is honored carries a lot of weight. In other words, we honor something or someone that we highly value. For example, we listen carefully to the words of a judge in court. In fact, we're called to rise in respect when the "honorable" judge enters the court. We even address a judge as "your Honor."

We place a great weight or value on words, persons or things of honor. So it should be with our parents: We should honor them. Children honor parents by responding to them in obedience and talking to them and treating them with respect and reverence. Children also honor their parents when they prove themselves to be trustworthy.

*Secrets of a Happy Family*

Children who learn obedience and humility have a good chance of becoming persons of honor. If children are truthful, their honesty brings great honor to their parents. If children affirm and build up others, they honor their parents greatly. When children are respectful to older persons, they bring honor to their parents.

Sheila's mother was being disorderly in the nursing home where she lived. Sheila felt guilty about putting her mother there, so she decided to bring her into her own home. The family was cautious but still friendly.

Sheila soon noticed a favorable change in her mother and came to discover that her mother was fearful of being returned to her childhood orphanage. Her mother had been alone as a child and didn't want to die alone in what seemed like an orphanage. In this way Sheila learned—in fact, her whole family learned—how to honor a person's spirit just by acknowledging who they are and their fears. Sheila's mother died a few years later with great dignity and much honor.

Frank was raised by his dad, who was his closest friend. Frank was athletic, and his dad always took time to go to his athletic events. When Frank was in high school, his dad was always there to encourage him, and at times he showed him where Scripture called for a change in Frank's attitude or behavior.

*The Role of the Children*

In college Frank met a wonderful girl named Sue. After college they married and taught their children God's Word as they both had learned from their parents. When Frank's dad's health became poor, and old age slowed him down to the point that he could no longer care for himself, Frank continued to honor his dad—just as he had done as a single young man and then as a married, middle-aged father.

Frank couldn't give his father the physical care he needed. After much prayer, he placed his dad in a nursing home. A day didn't pass without at least one member of the family visiting his dad, whether they felt like it or not.

This experience has taught Frank and his family that showing honor may involve doing painful or costly things to protect and help the one we honor. Frank's dad is still alive and doesn't recognize anyone, but reverence, obedience and honor are being expressed by Frank, his wife and their children. Their children certainly have been given an example of how to "honor thy father and mother" (Exodus 20:12).

Children trained to be obedient to parents and lawful authority have a high probability of becoming wise and productive adults. "When you walk, your step will not be impeded, and should you run, you will not stumble. Hold fast to instruction" (Proverbs 4:12-13). Children who learn to accept correction honor those who have taught them along the way.

*Secrets of a Happy Family*

Hank was a bright but rebellious young man who was in trouble much of the time. He did poorly in school, was often late for work, lost several jobs and got into alcohol. He came from a loving family, but he was too headstrong for them. He joined the army to get away from his problems and soon found himself in combat in a faraway country.

While there, he came to realize that the training he'd received as a child and now as a military man were similar. They both taught that obedience, humility and reverence are the very essence of experiencing the fullness of life. Hank came home from the war and began to use the talents that God had given him. He became a successful businessman and a spiritually mature father and grandfather. Hank's road to honor began a long time ago when he learned about God and obedience from his mother.

## Respect and reverence

Scripture tells us that all children are expected to have reverence and respect for their parents (see Leviticus 19:3). Even if our earthly mother and father abandon us, we are still to treat them with respect should we ever meet them. Reverence means "fear of the Lord." It can also mean being completely in awe of someone.

Reverence for God recalls that He created everything on this earth. We're not to be reverent because we fear that God is looking for ways to kill us. We're to be reverent because He is God, Creator of the universe. He is to be loved and respected for who He is.

Parents, because they are bearers of life, also deserve the reverence and respect of their children. We're called to have reverence for our parents because they gave us life. Even if our parents did nothing else for us but give us life, they still deserve our respect.

## Passing on the faith

As children develop, they learn how to revere their parents by way of example. Children learn how to worship from the way they experience it with their parents. If children are taken to church, left there until the service is over, then picked up again by a parent, they probably won't develop a hunger and reverence for God. The relationship children experience with their earthly fathers may very well establish the type of spiritual relationship they have with their heavenly Father. How can we expect children to revere their earthly father, when their earthly father doesn't revere his heavenly Father?

Chris was an intelligent, athletic and handsome young man. It seemed he had everything going for him, so it was a shock to everyone when he took his own life by hanging himself. But a deeper look into his life showed that his relationship with his father was damaged.

*Secrets of a Happy Family*

Apparently, this young man had believed he couldn't please his father with any of his achievements. He'd been criticized severely throughout his childhood and teen years. He'd developed a large chip on his shoulder, which had made him present to the world a mask of rebellion. In reality, however, he had been a warm, loving, lost young man.

Chris's mother was torn in two watching her son being cut down by his father inch by inch, day by day, year by year. Finally, the young man had had enough. In his view, there was no hope, so he ended his pain in a tragic way. This young man's father had little or no faith to hand on to his son. So he was incapable of reaching out to protect him from the danger of suicide and the possibility that he might face an eternity of darkness.

Children need to know that they're loved not for what they do or don't do, but because of what Jesus Christ did. That's why passing on the faith to the next generation is so important. Today we realize through God's holy Word and the teachings of the Church how much we are really loved. Through the power of God's love, many children have overcome the burden of being abandoned and rejected.

The need to be loved burns deeply in the heart of all children. Children whose parents lead them to the light of Christ are blessed indeed; God will honor such parents highly. Jesus Himself tells us that whatever we do to the least of

*The Role of the Children*

His brethren, we do to Him (see Matthew 25:31-46).

Today there is tremendous dishonor in our society in the way children are being treated. To honor our children we must first understand what it means to honor our own mother and father. Our children need more examples of honor in our churches, in our workplaces, in our schools and, of course, in our families. A child will likely honor his parents when he grows up in a home where parents share with their children what God teaches them in Sacred Scripture, and when they go to a church where godly men and women teach them how to live as Jesus did, thereby bringing honor to the family name. Our children need parents to show them by example that faith is the living response to the power and presence of God in their lives.

## Questions for Reflection

- How am I, as a child of God, showing reverence to my heavenly Father?
- How does my faith show my children the power and presence of God in my life?
- How can I listen more effectively in my desire to be obedient?

## Application of the Lesson

*Mark 9:7:* "This is my Son, my beloved. Listen to Him."

Read the Gospel text above. Meditate on it. Listen to what the Lord is saying to you, then obey it and talk about what He has said.

Let us pray.

Lord, You are our Father; we are Your children. We place our complete trust in Your loving care. We praise You and honor You, for you alone are worthy of praise. Amen.

## CHAPTER SEVEN
# THE ROLE OF THE HOLY SPIRIT

When Jesus went to sit at the right hand of the Father in heaven, He didn't leave us alone, but sent us his Holy Spirit to be with us. The Holy Spirit is here to comfort us, sanctify us, teach us and empower us. He comforts us when we're hurting. He sanctifies us, makes us holy, through our suffering. He teaches us through the Word of God and through the Church. He empowers us to be channels of healing to a battered, broken world and to be Jesus' witnesses.

### Sanctification

Sanctification is the process of becoming whole—that is, holy. Scripture tells us that Jesus was made perfect through suffering and obedience (see Hebrews 5:8). The *Catechism* says: "'Although he was a son, [Jesus] learned obedience through what he suffered.' How much more reason have we sinful creatures to learn obedience—we who in Him have become children of adoption" (par. 2825).

In becoming holy, the average man becomes infused by God's Holy Spirit and transformed for His service. Being holy means letting your daily lifestyle be an expression

*Secrets of a Happy Family*

of the Lord. The way we live clearly demonstrates what we believe.

If we believe that God really loves us, then our lives will bear witness to His saving grace. We'll forgive others simply because we've been forgiven by Him (see Matthew 6:14-15). We'll be able to share what we have and not feel pressured to follow the world's principle of "me first." To be concerned about others is to many a sign of weakness, but what you do to the weakest, you do to Christ Himself (see Matthew 25:31-46).

Sanctification is the change that God begins to make in our lives when we become Christians. It's experienced when we as believers yield to the presence and power of the Holy Spirit. The Holy Spirit then is able to produce certain character traits within us. By our own power, we can't just go out and practice these traits, which Scripture calls "fruit of the Spirit" (see Galatians 5:22-23): love, joy, peace, patience, kindness, goodness, faithfulness, gentleness and self-control. If we want the fruit of the Spirit to develop in our lives, we must recognize that all these characteristics are found in Christ, and the way to sanctification is to join our lives to His.

Commenting on the phrase of the Our Father "hallowed be Thy name," St. Cyprian once said: "By whom is God hallowed, since He is the one who hallows? But since He said, 'You shall be holy to me; for I the Lord am holy,' we

*The Role of the Holy Spirit*

seek and ask that we who were sanctified in baptism may persevere in what we have begun to be. And we ask this daily, for we need sanctification daily, so that we who fail daily may cleanse away our sins by being sanctified continually. . . . We pray that this sanctification may remain in us" (quoted in the *Catechism,* par. 2813).

We must always remember that God sanctifies us in the blood of His Son Jesus through the work of the Holy Spirit. "God it is who has given you life in Christ Jesus. He has made Him our wisdom and also our justice, our sanctification and our redemption" (1 Corinthians 1:30).

The *Bread of Life Catholic Bible Study* asks: "What leads us to righteousness and what must we do with our bodies to sanctify them?" The Scripture tells us that obedience leads to righteousness, and we must make our bodies servants of justice for our sanctification (see Romans 6:16-19). That means denying ourselves frivolous actions and things.

## God's Word

How do we become sanctified? Through God's Word, because His Word is His sanctifying agent. The Word convicts us and brings about a change in us by stripping us of ego, (see Luke 9:23) and allowing us to think more of others than ourselves (see Philippians 2:2-4).

We must renew this commitment to God's Word daily. We can't do God's work when we're filled with our own ego.

*Secrets of a Happy Family*

Doing God's work means dying to our ego for the sake of others. Sanctification is part of each believer's experience—in other words, his story—and becoming a witness is the best way to tell that story. The goal of that sanctification is preparing and sending believers into the world to glorify God by doing His work (see John 17:17-19).

## Faith

What we believe is demonstrated by the amount of faith we have. Faith is a gift to us from God. All we have to do is accept the gift.

In simplified terms, "faith, then, comes through hearing, and what is heard is the Word of Christ" (Romans 10:17). We can deepen this gift of faith by asking the Holy Spirit to increase it as He teaches us how to apply the Word of God to our everyday lives. Our part is to listen when He speaks and obey whatever He tells us. As we become more in tune to His voice, whether it's through the Bible or through the teachings of the Church, our faith will increase.

When Bill read in the Scriptures that everyone should be slow to speak, slow to anger and quick to listen (see James 1:19), he was convicted of his failure to live up to this standard. Bill typically dominated conversations and listened little. His wife had told him many times before about this problem, but it took the power of God's Word to change him.

## The Role of the Holy Spirit

Scripture tells us that an unbelieving spouse can be sanctified by the believing spouse (see 1 Corinthians 7:14). Jenny lives as a loving Christian woman with her husband, a nonbeliever. Her attitude and behavior tells him what Scripture means to her. She rises earlier than her husband to spend time alone with the Lord and to pray for him. She reads Scripture every chance she can and tries to live in accordance with the Scriptures, especially in loving her husband.

She can't talk about her love for the Lord with him because he doesn't want to hear it, and this is painful for her. But she shares her love for the Lord through service to her husband and loving him as he is. She preaches God's holy Word to her husband through her actions rather than her tongue. Her husband is deeply impressed by her faith in God.

"You married women must obey your husbands, so that any of them who do not believe in the word of the gospel may be won over apart from preaching, through their wives' conduct. They have only to observe the reverent purity of your way of life. The affectation of an elaborate hair dress, the wearing of golden jewelry, or the donning of rich robes is not for you. Your adornment is rather the hidden character of the heart, expressed in the unfading beauty of a calm and gentle disposition. This is precious in God's eyes. The holy women of past ages used to adorn themselves in this way, reliant on God and obedient to their husbands—for example,

Sarah, who was subject to Abraham and called him her master" (1 Peter 3:1-6).

## The Blood of Christ

Sanctification, we've said, is effected by the Holy Spirit, and the Word of God is an active agent in the process of salvation and healing. Scripture insists that the blood of Christ provides the basis for God's sanctification of believers. The book of Hebrews tells us: "For if the blood of goats and bulls and the sprinkling of a heifer's ashes can sanctify those who are defiled so that their flesh is cleansed, how much more will the blood of Christ, who through the eternal Spirit offered Himself up unblemished to God, cleanse our consciences from dead works to worship the living God" (9:13-14).

The blood sprinkled on us, who are sinners, cleanses our consciences from acts that lead to death. His blood washed us clean and took away the guilt of our sins. All wrongdoing and disobedience to God's Word leads to death. He has sanctified us by spilling His blood so that we may serve Him and live forever.

## The Word Is Truth

Jesus prayed to the Father, "Consecrate them by means of truth; your Word is truth" (John 17:17). His Word sanctifies us by the power of the Holy Spirit. We're sanctified

## The Role of the Holy Spirit

by the Holy Spirit so that we can serve the living God. As the *Catechism* notes: "The Spirit who teaches the Church and recalls for her everything that Jesus said was also to form her in the life of prayer" (par. 2623).

If we're sanctified by means of the truth, and God's Word is truth, it follows that we should be reading and studying His Word so that He can sanctify us and make us holy. Conversion is not a one-time event. It's a process of sanctification through an ever-growing desire to serve Him. He sanctifies us through His Word, and as we come to know the truth, we come to know Jesus, who is the Truth. He is the Way, the Truth, and the Life.

Our believing and accepting Him becomes apparent by the way we act upon the Word. Service to others is the proof of what we believe—service with a heart of joy and love for our fellow man. If we say we believe and aren't serving our fellow man, we're lying.

Martha is consecrated daily as she reads God's Word. In the readings of the day, the Lord always speaks a special word to her. Many times He helps her to see a truth that will bring her into repentance. He's then able to use her to serve Him.

One scriptural text that has brought Martha to the truth and has sanctified her is 1 Corinthians chapter 13. There, St. Paul tells us that love is patient and kind.

*Secrets of a Happy Family*

One day, when Martha's children were fighting, she shouted at them in anger, grabbed each one by the arm, shook them, and sent them to their rooms. Later, when she read 1 Corinthians 13, it convicted her and brought her to repentance. She went to the children and asked them to forgive her for her impatience. She then led the children in prayer, asking God to help them to love and not fight with each other. She also asked God to give their mommy patience with her children, just as Jesus is patient with her.

## Power in the Spirit

As we've noted, Ken has suffered from a chronic lung disease since birth. He also struggles with rheumatoid arthritis, chronic prostatitis and asthma. He has to pray for the strength to endure the pain that goes with his afflictions. He drives himself on with passion and conviction that he will someday be healed. He wants to encourage others not to give up by his own witness. He tries to respond to anyone who calls for help.

Nevertheless, Ken sometimes grows weary in his own suffering, and at times he seems to be losing his inner fire. The pain that used to irritate him now seems at times almost too much to bear. He wakes up in pain and goes to bed in pain. He finds at times that he can't even breathe and must rely on an oxygen tank.

*The Role of the Holy Spirit*

At times, Ken falls into self-pity when Satan tries to depress his spirit. But Ken realizes that as long as he yields to the power of the Holy Spirit within him and joins his own suffering with the suffering of Christ, he can make it. He knows that with Christ nothing is impossible (see Philippians 4:13).

Ken must rely heavily on the power of the Holy Spirit working through him. He loves to call on God's Word when he's facing a great deal of pain. Scripture tells him that Jesus is the source of supply for all his needs (see Philippians 4:19). This is a tremendous comfort in his time of pain, and Jesus always comes to him to supply his needs through prayer, rest, sleep or just letting the power of His Word comfort him physically, emotionally, and spiritually.

Recently, while being treated for a prostate problem, Ken discovered that he was also dealing with a painful hernia in the groin. Then as before, God's Word gave him hope and strength. God has blessed Ken physically many times, and through the power of the Holy Spirit, he has experienced major healing in his body.

Ken once read in Scripture that St. Paul asked the Lord to take away a "thorn" in his side—some kind of affliction. But the thorn was there to keep him from becoming proud and pompous (see 2 Corinthians 12:7-10). Marie suggested that this could possibly be the same reason why Ken wasn't being completely healed. The moment of truth had come for Ken. After much stuttering and posturing, he had to agree with her.

We prayed right then and there that Ken would accept God's will and God's plan for his healing and ministry. Now Ken has come to accept his weakness so that God can work through him, and this has brought him a deep sense of peace. The Lord said to St. Paul, "My grace is enough for you, for in weakness power reaches perfection" (2 Corinthians 12:9). Paul's response to God was that he would gladly boast of his weaknesses so that the power of Christ might rest upon him. Ken, too, is now boasting of his weaknesses so that the power of Christ may rest upon him.

## Comforter

The Holy Spirit is our Comforter. He comforts us in all our afflictions. Jesus said He would not leave us orphaned. When He ascended to the Father in heaven, He left us His Spirit to be our Comforter, especially in times of trial. "He comforts us in all our afflictions and thus enables us to comfort those who are in trouble with the same consolation we have received from Him" (2 Corinthians 1:4).

God comforts Ken in his affliction and gives him His grace so that he can comfort others in their afflictions. When Ken is powerless, it's then that he is strong (see 2 Corinthians 12:10). Ken now thanks God for al-

## The Role of the Holy Spirit

lowing him to come to this point in his life where nothing else matters as much as his relationship with Jesus. That's what it means when the Lord tells us that His grace is sufficient for us.

So many times people who suffer a lot have a terrific opportunity to serve the Lord. They can yield to the power of the Holy Spirit, who will bring about healing. Sometimes the healing is emotional, spiritual or even physical. Ken now realizes all this, and he thanks God every night for all the chances he has to lead someone to Christ through his weakness during the day.

Recently Ken was having difficulty breathing as he climbed a knoll at the local cemetery. He was to do a graveside service for an infant. Not feeling well made him feel inadequate in performing this service. He prayed that God's power would help him in his own weakness and let him bring comfort and consolation to the family of this little child.

As Ken approached the graveside, he reached out and hugged the grieving young parents. He told them that the sorrow would pass with time, but love lasts forever. Ken reminded them that the pain would pass, but the memory of the child and their love for her would always be in their hearts. Ken left the cemetery knowing that God's grace would be sufficient for this grieving family as well as for himself.

*Secrets of a Happy Family*

In Scripture the Holy Spirit is called the *Paraclete,* which means literally "one called alongside to help." He's also called the Advocate, Helper, and Comforter. This means that the Holy Spirit isn't here to do things we should rightfully be doing ourselves. He's here to come alongside to help us, to give us comfort and support.

The Holy Spirit is power, and when we're baptized in the Spirit, we receive the power of the Spirit. We receive the Father, Son and Holy Spirit in our baptism. As we receive the gift of the Holy Spirit, His power within us is released. We become temples of the Holy Spirit (see 1 Corinthians 6:19) and are graced with His presence residing in our temple, our body.

Jesus told us on the cross that He thirsts for us (see John 19:28), that He yearns for our love, especially in our time of pain. Let's go to Him when we're in pain; He will supply us with life-giving water. Look for people who are in pain and who thirst for God's comfort and living water (see John 4:14). Through the power of the Holy Spirit and the healing blood of Christ, we can bring comfort to them, allowing them to be washed free of sin and affliction.

## Teacher

Jesus told His disciples that "the Paraclete, the Holy Spirit whom the Father will send in my name, will instruct you in everything, and remind you of all that I told you"

## The Role of the Holy Spirit

(John 14:26). Our Teacher is the Holy Spirit. He teaches us through His Word and through the Church. We who have accepted and believed in Jesus Christ are the Church; we are His disciples today.

Jesus promised the disciples that the Holy Spirit would help them remember what He had taught them. We can be confident that the Gospels are accurate records of what Jesus taught and did. The power of the Holy Spirit helped the disciples remember what they saw and heard. Today, the Holy Spirit comes alongside us to inspire and encourage us to learn more about Jesus, and then to go out and proclaim Him to the world. Scripture is good for teaching (see 2 Timothy 3:16), and the Holy Spirit is our Teacher (see John 14:26).

When we allow the Holy Spirit to come into our temple and become our Paraclete or Comforter, He gives us a keen sense of lasting peace. The impact of the Holy Spirit's role as a Teacher is reflected in the power of the Word and Church. The Word becomes powerful when it is lived out, and the Holy Spirit is the power that brings on the change in our lives.

In the past, Marie had always recognized others as superior to herself, but not in the sense of Philippians 2:3, which says: "Never act out of rivalry or conceit; rather, let all parties thing humbly of others as superior to themselves." Instead, Marie simply felt inferior to others. As a child Marie had suffered from a learning disability. She began her school years with difficulty understanding what was being taught. Her education was a struggle and added to her sense of inferiority. Her teachers also discovered that she couldn't see well.

But Marie's life was changed when she learned from the Holy Spirit that God loved her and sent His Son Jesus to die for her, thus proving His love for her. She began to recognize the Holy Spirit as her Teacher and the third Person of the Blessed Trinity who had taken up residence in her life, who would teach her everything she needed to know to live the abundant life. When the Lord revealed Himself this way, and the inner voice of God's Spirit told her that He was her Teacher and He would teach her how to love, she was overjoyed.

She had never realized that God's Spirit was her Teacher. She had always thought that others' teaching ability came from hard work, studying and accomplishments. She'd assumed that if she applied herself enough, she too could learn. Yet no matter how hard she'd tried, she just hadn't felt accepted and hadn't achieved what she'd hoped to achieve.

When the Lord revealed Himself to her, she developed a hunger to know Jesus personally through the Bible. Now she reads it every day, and God speaks to her every day. He reveals His love for her, and she feels more and more loved. She's now capable of loving those she comes

## The Role of the Holy Spirit

in contact with, even those who aren't loving to her.

Marie says a prayer to God before she reads the Word, telling God that she can't understand His Word without His grace. She acknowledges her own weakness before Him in order not to become proud and to rely on her own ability. She acknowledges her weakness so that His power can reach perfection in her. She asks Him to send His Holy Spirit to remind, teach, and guide her to the truth (see John 14:26). The Truth, she knows, is Jesus; He is the Way, the Truth, and the Life (see John 14:6). She asks all this in order to share with others everything He teaches her.

As Marie shares with others and yields to His Holy Spirit, she then becomes the mouthpiece of God. She becomes the hands, feet and heart of God by sharing the good news of what Jesus is doing in her life. He then begins to teach others using her as His mouthpiece. As she hears others in the Church preaching and teaching, she recognizes Him speaking and teaching her through them.

Now that Marie has come to know Jesus personally in the Word, she is frequently able to discern when He's teaching and speaking to her through another person, or when another person is simply speaking his own thoughts. False teachers abound, so it's extremely important for us to know and recognize God's voice. We do this by yielding to Him, listening to Him and obeying Him.

The Holy Spirit taught Marie that she can't isolate herself from others with an attitude of "just me and God"; she needs to be part of a Christian community, the Church. To stay under the authority of the Church is to stay under the authority of Christ.

## Empowerment

Scripture tells us, "When the Holy Spirit has come upon you, you will receive power to testify about me with great effect, to the people in Jerusalem, throughout Judea, in Samaria, and to the ends of the earth, about my death and Resurrection" (Acts 1:8). The *Catechism* adds: "This love (the charity of 1 Corinthians 13) is the source of the new life in Christ, made possible because we have received 'power' from the Holy Spirit. By this power of the Spirit, God's children can bear much fruit" (par. 735, 736).

The power that comes from the Holy Spirit was not limited to the Apostles. This power has been handed down to all who believe in Jesus Christ right up until today. All who believe can experience the healing power of the Holy Spirit in their daily lives.

Many believers, however, haven't fully realized that we are temples of the Holy Spirit (see 1 Corinthians 6:19) and possess a power residing within us. The Holy Spirit residing in us as temples is the same Spirit who was present to the Apostles. Because of our gift of free will, we have a

## The Role of the Holy Spirit

choice about whether to release the power of the Holy Spirit within us.

We carry the presence of Christ wherever we go. We are Christ-bearers, and the ground beneath us becomes holy because of Who we bear.

Scripture tells us that when we receive the Spirit, power will come upon us (see Acts 1:8). Within our breast lies more power than a thousand hydrogen bombs. The power of the Holy Spirit grows within us as we call upon the Spirit and, in Jesus' name, use that power.

Jesus promised that when His believers received the Holy Spirit, they would have the power to go out and witness in His name to the ends of the earth. We can't witness in His name with power if we haven't received the Holy Spirit. At the same time, the power of the Holy Spirit can be blocked and slowed down by sin.

A major artery to the heart must carry a clean, open, unobstructed flow of blood if the heart is to be healthy. If the artery is clogged, the blood clots prevent the blood from flowing into the heart chamber freely. This may cause severe damage or even death.

In a similar way, sin is the clot that blocks the power of the Holy Spirit from being released. Many people aren't even aware that they're in great danger of having a spiritual heart attack. So it's important to remember that we bear witness to Christ, not to show God what we can do,

*Secrets of a Happy Family*

but to show and tell others what God has done for us.

We recently attended a Christian conference where a young lady appeared on the stage to sing. She came out in a wheelchair, having been paralyzed because of an accident years ago. The audience was filled with many handicapped people, and her presence had a dramatic impact.

When she began to sing, most of the crowd wept and cried out in joy. She was full of the Holy Spirit, and she was empowering the entire audience with her witness of hope. She shared her testimony and told the crowd not to have pity on her because she knew that His grace was sufficient for her. She knew that in her weakness was His strength.

When it was time for her to leave the stage, many handicapped people rushed forward in their own wheelchairs and begged her to share more of her experience with a God who promises and brings hope to His people. She encouraged others who were handicapped to trust in the Lord, reminding them that His grace is sufficient for them, too (see 2 Cor. 12:9-10).

God has empowered us through His Holy Spirit, and He wants us to empower others with our testimony of His presence in our lives. This witness must begin with our own families. Only when people are exposed to the truth can they ever really be free. They must be told that Jesus is the only way we can ever really be free (see John 8:32).

## The Role of the Holy Spirit

Divine empowerment lets ordinary people do extraordinary things. When Jesus died and rose from the dead, He empowered us all to live with Him forever and ever and to do extraordinary things. We must remember that Jesus was the only Man who was born to die to save the world. The Holy Spirit raised Him and empowered Him with life, and He continues to do that today for all believers.

The Holy Spirit empowers us to love one another as He has loved us, even when we ourselves aren't being loved by others. When we call on Him, He gives us the grace to respond to others with love. The Holy Spirit empowers men to become the spiritual leaders in their homes and communities. The Holy Spirit empowers women to become affirmers and supporters of others. The Holy Spirit empowers couples to be united as one in Christ. The Holy Spirit empowers parents to be co-creators. The Holy Spirit empowers single persons to reflect His image. The Holy Spirit empowers children to be obedient. The Holy Spirit empowers all believers to be His witnesses.

The biblical word for *witness* literally means "martyr": one who dies for others, just as Jesus did. A witness is one who follows in the Master's footsteps. Thus those who empty themselves of self and become vessels of love, a container of God, are also martyrs.

The harvest is great and the laborers are few. Why not ask the harvest Master to help you to die to your ego so that you can be one of the laborers who have joined the great harvest?

We began this book talking about God's love because we believe you cannot have a loving relationship with others until you come to know and receive the love and forgiveness that God is offering to you through His beloved Son, Jesus Christ. We end this book by encouraging you to allow the power of the Holy Spirit in you to change transform, and renew the face of the earth.

## Questions for Reflection

- How do I go about dying to my ego?
- What do I need to do to have more power in my life?
- What has the Holy Spirit taught me this week?

## Application of the Lesson

*1 Corinthians 6:19:* "You must know that your body is a temple of the Holy Spirit, who is within—the Spirit you have received from God. You are not your own."

Recall a situation in which your body was used to glorify God. Think of a specific time when you chose to stop doing something that would degrade your body.

Let us pray:

Holy Spirit, thank You for all you have taught me and for all that You will teach me in the days to come. You are my Comforter, Refuge, Guide, Deliverer. I love You with all my heart. Amen.

# SEMINAR SUGGESTIONS

## GOD'S DIVINE ORDER FOR THE FAMILY
## Seven-Week Seminar

### Two-Hour Sessions

7:00 p.m.  *Week One:* God's Love
Opening Prayer
Introduction

7:10 p.m.  Talk on God's love and the meaning of love in today's society. Include in the presentation material from chapter one, Scripture, encyclicals, and the *Catechism of the Catholic Church.*

7:40 p.m.  Quiet reflection (questions from the end of the chapter)

8:00 p.m.  Couple Discussion (sharing about the presentation and your personal reflections)

8:30 p.m.  Give overview of talk. Present the application of the lesson for this week that appears at the end of each chapter.

8:40 p.m.  Social time

9:00 p.m.  Closing Prayers (you can use the one at end of each chapter)

*Secrets of a Happy Family*

For the following six weeks, use the same format, except add ten minutes after the opening prayer with sharing by two couples on how they implemented the homework.

End the seminar in the power of the Holy Spirit, asking Him to equip them with something far beyond anything they could have imagined. God loves us and has given us His Holy Spirit to be with us always.

# NOTES

1. Pope John Paul II, *Familiaris Consortio (Apostolic Exhortation on the Family)*, 18, December 15, 1981.
2. Pope John Paul II, Encyclical *Redemptor Hominis*, 10: AAS 71 (1979), 274.
3. *Familiaris Consortio*, 13.
4. See Ephesians 3:15.
5. See Second Vatican Council, *Gaudium et Spes*, 52.
6. *Familiaris Consortio*, 25.
7. *Familiaris Consortio*, 63.
8. *Familiaris Consortio*, 22.
9. *Familiaris Consortio*, 22.
10. *Familiaris Consortio*, 22.
11. *Familiaris Consortio*, 28.
12. *Familiaris Consortio*, 83.
13. *Familiaris Consortio*, 27.
14. *Familiaris Consortio*, 27.